T0267076

# DONE BEING SINGLE

A LATE BLOOMER'S
GUIDE TO LOVE

# DONE BEING SINGLE

TREVA BRANDON
SCHARF

GREENLEAF
BOOK GROUP PRESS

Published by Greenleaf Book Group Press
Austin, Texas
www.gbgpress.com

Distributed by Greenleaf Book Group

For ordering information or special discounts for bulk purchases, please contact Greenleaf Book Group at PO Box 91869, Austin, TX 78709, 512.891.6100.

Design and composition by Greenleaf Book Group
Cover design by Greenleaf Book Group
Cover Images: ©Shutterstock/therealtakeone; desthrashx; Vectorcreator

Publisher's Cataloging-in-Publication data is available.

Print ISBN: 979-8-88645-020-0

eBook ISBN: 979-8-88645-021-7

To offset the number of trees consumed in the printing of our books, Greenleaf donates a portion of the proceeds from each printing to the Arbor Day Foundation. Greenleaf Book Group has replaced over 50,000 trees since 2007.

Printed in the United States of America on acid-free paper

23  24  25  26  27  28  29    11  10  9  8  7  6  5  4  3  2

First Edition

*To Robby,*
*My late-blooming groom,*
*muse, trophy husband, the G.O.A.T.*

# CONTENTS

# INTRODUCTION

*I was a late bloomer. But anyone who blooms*
*at all, ever, is very lucky.*

—Sharon Olds

Still not married and in my late 40s, you could say I was either a late bloomer, unlucky in love, too picky, or a confirmed bachelorette. Actually, I was a little of each until I turned 50. That's when my long, strange trip through singlehood finally ended, and an even stranger trip would begin: my life as a first-time midlife wife.

Before I got married, I had more than paid my dues in the dating world. I had countless romances and relationships, boyfriends and breakups, heartaches and heartbreaks. I loved and lost, dumped and got dumped, was victim and villain. I took some hard knocks and threw a few knockout punches. I saw it all, dated it all, and lived to tell.

Then, literally on my 50th birthday in 2013, I met a most interesting creature who would change my life forever: a fellow late bloomer named Robby Scharf. Then 56 years old and never married either, Robby was everything I had been waiting 50 years for: a true love, the real deal, and someone who was all-in when it came to being with me.

Robby and I got engaged six months after our first date, and the following year, in 2014, I walked down the aisle at 51.

Right after we got engaged, I started my blog *The Late-Blooming Bride* as a way to chronicle my journey from singleton to spouse, with all the hard-won wisdom I gained along the way. Getting married for the first time at 51 made for a good story: It was a tale with humor and hope, and it had to be told.

At first, my blogs were about the weirdness of getting married in your 50s, with titles like "Wedding Plans-A-Palooza," "Welcome to Registry Hell," and "Women Are from Venus, Men Are from Costco."

After a while, though, I found myself writing more serious pieces about surviving singlehood, navigating the dating world, reclaiming your power in relationships, and being an empowered woman at any age. As my life evolved, so did my blog titles: "Put Yourself on Your Own Damn Pedestal," "One Day You'll Thank the Ex Who Dumped You," "Vulnerability Is the New Black," and "Stop Waiting for People to Love You."

As I found my voice, my message started to resonate, and my audience grew. This led to all kinds of invitations for interviews, podcast appearances, online summits, women's conferences, and panel discussions. As a result, I became somewhat of a post-50s authority in the midlife dating space and an advocate for strong, independent women everywhere. Whether I'm blogging, dispensing dating advice, or telling my own story, I speak my mind and don't hold back. Nothing is sacred, and there is no such thing as TMI.

When a producer at VoiceAmerica Talk Radio Network approached me to see if I'd be interested in turning my TMI into a podcast, I jumped at the chance— but with one condition: I cohost it with my husband. I recruited Robby for the male point of view, and in 2017 we created *Done Being Single*, the podcast. Full credit goes to Robby for the title, but we both agreed on what it meant to be "done." When you're done being single you're done looking, done settling for crumbs, done with drama, and done putting up with less than you deserve. When coming up with a title for this book, all I had to remember was that moment when Robby and I were done being single, and the rest is history.

Along with sharing our marital adventures and exploits on our podcast, we interviewed heavy-hitters in the personal growth and relationship space, including *New York Times* bestselling authors, TED Talk speakers, acclaimed relationship experts, and thought leaders in the areas of love and dating, to supplement what we didn't know. Even I, a professional single who thought she knew everything about dating, was schooled. I was so impressed, in fact, that I've included in this book original quotes from some of our podcast guests such as John Gray, author of *Men Are from Mars, Women Are from Venus*; psychotherapist, author, and TED Talk Speaker Lori Gottlieb; and Arielle Ford, bestselling author known for her teachings on the law of attraction.

Forget about love-bombing, ghosting, and other staples of dating—it wasn't until I learned about evolutionary psychology, attachment theory, upper limit problems, the five love languages, adjustment shock, and imposter syndrome that my mind was officially blown. When I stumbled upon the genius of social scientist Brené Brown, the keen insights of social observer Malcolm Gladwell, and the wisdom of the ancient Greek Stoics, I had to include them in my book, too. They're the rock stars of the dating world, even though they have nothing to do with dating. Unbeknownst to them, their wisdom actually has everything to do with dating, being single, and finding love, because it's based on self-reliance and empowerment—which to me is the basis of dating, being single, and finding love.

All of them, plus the brilliant bloggers I follow and my own research on love, have taught me that dating is scientific and personal growth is sexy, and it's all woven into my life and this book.

My blogs and podcast, although real and raw, only scratched the surface. There was more to the story, and much more I wanted to say, so I decided to go deeper. This book is the result. It's my tell-all, with all the dirt, untold stories, and never-been-published moments of my 51-year single-to-married world tour. You won't see it in an article or interview, or hear it on a podcast; it's that personal and private.

## THE TELL-ALL THAT HELPS ALL

I like to think of this book as a memoir, a singles survival guide, a dating handbook for millennials, a morale boost for midlifers, a love letter to late bloomers, and an operating manual for anyone at any age looking to achieve their personal best in life and love. Which means if you're freaking out in your 20s, hyperventilating in your 30s, or living a life of not-so-quiet desperation in your 40s (like I was), I've got you covered.

*Done Being Single: A Later Bloomer's Guide to Love* is my look back on single life, which means that before putting pen to paper I had years to figure it out, years to screw it up, and more years to eventually get it right. I'm no angel, and far from perfect. I made every mistake in the book, in fact, I wrote the damn book—and this is it.

Writing this book was a tough job, but someone had to do it. Someone had to be single all those years to unlock the secrets. I may not be the oldest first-time bride, but I do have a lot to say about it. Not only did my long road to the altar give me some great dating fodder, it gave me some great lessons about resilience and grit—things I needed growing up as an only child, things I needed going solo as a single woman, things I needed trying to get pregnant on my own, and things I needed many years later when I faced love and loss in the time of coronavirus.

## WHO I AM

In addition to sharing my insights and dating trade secrets with you, I'm also going to challenge your old patterns, test your current thinking, and kick your ass in the process. Aside from being a dating expert, I'm a lifelong athlete and fitness professional with more than 40 years of exercise experience under my belt. I'm a USTA 4.0 doubles player, a CBVA beach volleyball player, a five-time marathoner, and a hardcore mah-jongg player—the most grueling sport of all.

I'm a tough-as-nails trainer and a never-say-quit athlete, a highly empathetic badass who is nicely flawed and deeply human, with issues just like anyone else; just ask my therapist (who's going to have a field day when he reads what's in here). I also study astrology and bet on sports, which means I'm just enough New Age and degenerate gambler to make things interesting.

I'm brutally honest and I don't sugar-coat. And yes, I eat sugar. I also drink, smoke pot, and curse. Warning: There will be F-bombs dropped throughout this book; just telling you now.

From my years in the fitness business to my years living single, to my life as an only child, I've got the kind of unique perspective that can only come from someone who's toughed it out in all worlds. I've also tapped into my expertise as a life/dating/relationship coach to round out the ass-kicking. In this book I am going to teach you what I teach my clients about the power of surrender, the benefits of breakups, the upside to waiting, and the key to finding your greatness.

I've also thrown in some pro tips and test-driven takeaways to date smarter, build resilience, and honor your highest good.

Even though I've racked up enough hours to call myself a dating expert, I'm only one woman's opinion. I'm not the last word on love, and I don't have all the answers. What I do have is the inside track on how to find a healthy relationship. Spoiler alert: turns out you need a healthy one with yourself first.

From interviewing smart people to gleaning insights from my own past experiences, observations, and professional training, I know what it takes to attract good people, good love, and be good at keeping both. There's still much to learn and I continue to be a student in many ways—but the journey is too good not to share, so I'm bringing you along with me.

Packed with life lessons, dating wisdom, sports analogies, and menopause rants, I like to think there's something for everyone in this book. It doesn't matter if you're a late bloomer or early blossomer; male or female, single or partnered. It doesn't matter if you're divorced, widowed, new on the market, stuck in dating hell, dreaming of getting married, or just dreaming of getting laid. Whoever you are, hopefully *Done Being Single: A Late Bloomer's Guide to Love* will give you what you need for your journey: hope, inspiration, tough love, and practical advice on how not to fuck it all up.

# POST-50 AND
# RIGHT ON TIME

*It does not matter how slowly you*
*go as long as you do not stop.*

—Confucius

T his was supposed to be the plan: meet a nice Jewish guy in my 20s (early 30s at the latest), date for a couple years, get married, have a big wedding, move into a white-picket-fence house in some upscale neighborhood in West LA, have a few kids, quit whatever job I had to become a soccer mom, a lady who lunches, and a full-time wife to my suit-and-tie banker, lawyer, or doctor husband.

As a child born in the early 1960s, I, along with countless girls of my era, bought into the social and cultural norms about love and marriage, along with the timelines and expectations that came with them. Back then it was a foregone conclusion you'd get married at a designated time, to a designated person, according to a designated plan.

But that didn't happen for me. It didn't happen in my 20s, 30s, or even in my 40s. As my mid-40s crept into late 40s, I knew there was a problem. There's no technical term for it, so I made one up:

I had late-onset marriage.

Having late-onset marriage meant that the husband, wedding, white-picket-fence house, and kids would all have to wait. The married life I was supposed to have wasn't happening—and might not happen at all—so I had no other choice than to go to Plan B. What was Plan B, you ask? Realizing this was going to take a while, so I had better get on it.

Plan B wasn't what I dreamed of, not what my parents wanted, and not what anyone expected. If there had been a Vegas sports betting line in 1963 on my wedding date and you laid down 50 bucks on the over/under, you'd be a gazillionaire right now. No one ever thought I'd be so late to my own wedding, let alone the oddsmakers.

As I like to say, I didn't choose to get married at 51. It chose me.

The odds of me getting hitched after 50 weren't good, and *Newsweek* magazine confirmed that with a story in 1986. The article carried the headline "Too Late for Prince Charming?" and included an alarming prediction: "It's easier to be killed by a terrorist than it is to find a husband if you're over the age of 40." Ironically, as I recall this pop culture meme, it has occurred to me that we're actually living in a world where you could be killed by a terrorist easier than you could find a husband after 40. It set off mass hysteria and panic for single women everywhere.[1] The article has been debated and debunked so many times over the years that *Newsweek* eventually retracted it. The trauma that ensued is still fresh in my mind.

I was 23 when the article came out, a year out of college and living in New York City at the time, with a bright future ahead of me and marriage somewhere on the horizon. I saw the hysteria the story caused, but didn't get hysterical, nor did I get the panic memo. Who were these women who couldn't get married? I naively thought that all women could get married when they wanted, regardless of age. My thinking was "Of course I'm going to get married one day, so why hurry? I'm young, attractive, and there's a whole world of guys who will want to marry me. I've got my pick." Ha! Little did I know it would apply to me many years later, when the panic finally set in, and I no longer had my pick. Last laugh on me.

---

1    See a follow-up article by Megan Garber, "When *Newsweek* 'Struck Terror in the Hearts of Single Women,'" *The Atlantic*, June 2, 2016, https://www.theatlantic.com/entertainment/archive/2016/06/more-likely-to-be-killed-by-a-terrorist-than-to-get-married/485171/.

## MARCHING TO A DIFFERENT DRUMMER

I didn't set out to be a late bloomer or a late-blooming bride, but here I am writing this book as both. It only took me 50 years, but according to my schedule, I'm right on time.

That's how we late bloomers roll. We take our time, march to the beat of our own drummers, and follow our own cadence and tempo, regardless of the rhythm around us. We go at our own pace. Our success can be slow-going, or sometimes not at all. Our greatest asset is patience; so is our greatest challenge. Our destinations may be different, but our journeys are the same: We get to where we're going just a little later than most.

Being late is the story of my life—maybe it's your story too.

There are all kinds of definitions of late bloomer, but my favorite is "an adult whose talent or genius appears later in life."

## All Sorts of Late Bloomers

If you didn't come into your own till after 40, there's a chance you might be a late bloomer. See if this sounds familiar:

- You were the last of your friends to lose your virginity or experience puberty.
- You might have had an awkward phase growing up.
- You know how to be patient.
- Your rites of passage came late, and your timeline got thrown out the window.
- You didn't misbehave until your late teens or early 20s (or even 30s and 40s, like me).
- You didn't follow the crowd.
- You didn't put a deadline on life experiences.
- You were impervious to peer pressure.

I'm no genius, but when it comes to getting married, I do feel there was a kind of unintended genius by waiting. Waiting gave me ample time to figure out who

I was and what I wanted (and didn't want, which is just as important). Waiting allowed me to tie up loose ends, resolve old issues, and get emotionally healthy. Waiting taught me to appreciate the insights a late-blooming life can give. Waiting also spared me the mistake of marrying the wrong person.

But the truth is, everyone is a late bloomer in some way; we're all a work in progress, and we blossom a little bit more every day. The learning, growing, and evolving never stop.

Late bloomer or no late bloomer, there's nothing wrong with taking your time, especially when it comes to love. Taking your time allows you to be more discerning about whom you date and let into your life. Plus, it gives you more time to weed out the riff-raff.

When I was single, I must've cleared a thousand acres of dating riff-raff before I could even see what I wanted. Just to be sure, I went out with all kinds: Average Joes, Prince Charmings, Peter Pans, confirmed bachelors, nerds, titans of industry, unemployed actors, and guys you bring home to Mother.

I was an equal opportunity dater whose dating life was like a cross between an international food court and a Hometown Buffet.

At the same time I was plowing through dates, I was plowing through jobs, trying to figure out what I wanted to be. One could also say waiting spared me the mistake of marrying the wrong person.

My first job was in advertising, where I discovered my knack for writing. In New York, I worked my way up from creative assistant to copywriter at ad agency BBDO. My early writing assignments included salad bar hangers for Pizza Hut, print campaigns for Pepsi, and trade ads for Visa. After five years, I moved back to Los Angeles and continued working in advertising. I wrote menu copy for Baja Fresh, online banners for Martha Stewart, liner notes and press releases for a record company, web copy for assisted living facilities, on-air promos for urban comedies, and movie posters for studios. I've also written reality TV content, feature film scripts, blogs, and now, a self-help memoir.

I was a true freelancer in every sense of the word, in that I never stayed with one gig or guy for that long. One could say I had job and relationship ADHD. As a result, it was hard getting traction in any one area. So in addition to having lousy timing, I had even worse staying power.

I hadn't met the right guy, and the fact that I was too self-reliant and independent (if that's even a thing) didn't help. I'm an Aquarius, and we prize our independence. I also have a Capricorn rising and a Virgo moon, so I'm a hard worker, but have a neurotic side. I'm obsessively organized, analytical, picky, and controlling. My closets and drawers are color-coded, my bra and underwear always match, and clutter sends me into a mental tailspin. I'm also claustrophobic, so small spaces and settling tend to freak me out.

I realized that the need for constant change—and slowness—had become a pattern, and not a productive one, and yet I felt helpless to do anything about it. The wiring was already installed, and the die cast. Was it some kind of pathology? A personality quirk? My parents' failed marriage and angst-ridden divorce? Or maybe it was my high tolerance for being on my own that played a part in my romantic life failing to launch in a timely manner.

Regardless of reason or cause, I ended up being late to just about all of life's important dates.

## FINDING YOUR GROOVE LATER IN LIFE

Ask a late bloomer and they'll probably tell you everything takes too damn long. Maybe because we have a tricky relationship with time—it either moves too slow, or it gets away from us altogether. Both were the case for me.

As my 40s closed in on 50, with so many failed relationships and go-nowhere romances, I became more despondent. I convinced myself I was over-the-dating-hill and no one would ever want someone at my age. My despondency turned into my worst fear: That *Newsweek* article was right, I was never going to find a husband, and was SOL, or shit out of luck, as they say.

That's a common belief for late bloomers (and midlifers too): If we haven't achieved something by 50, we're SOL. That includes marriage, remarriage, professional accomplishment, and success in general.

It's bad enough we feel that way—and it's even worse when the world sees us that way. The worry of ageism keeps a lot of us up at night, not just late bloomers. Turning 50 opened my eyes to an uncomfortable truth: You hit 50 at a time and in a world that doesn't really elevate people (especially women) of a certain age. The cruel irony is that just as you arrive, launch your second act, reinvent, start over, or get started, you're seen as too late to be taken seriously or even considered. All those years you spend perfecting and practicing, and accumulating wisdom, and the world tells you you're past your expiration date.

Unfortunately, ageism happens every day, in every medium, in every office, in every industry. Ageism even happens in dating apps. All you have to see is a commercial for a post-50 dating site to know what I'm talking about. Everything is old and stodgy, from the fake stock photo couples to the middle-aged singles pretending they've never heard of online dating. *Eye roll*. Every time I see one of these spots, I want to spit out my Geritol.

To my post-50 brothers and sisters out there: You may be older, but you're not over. Age is what you make of it, and greatness can happen no matter how old you are. If people can't see your value, they don't know value. If they can't see your worth, they don't know worth. I say this especially to men who don't date age-appropriate women. You have no idea what you're missing. We're hot, smart, sexy, and know who the Beatles are.

What makes the difference between sinking into midlife despair and laughing in its face is having a "growth mindset" instead of a fixed one. A growth mindset keeps moving and believing; a fixed mindset stays stuck. As Stanford University psychology professor Carol Dweck says in her book *Mindset: The New Psychology of Success*, "It's the difference between believing you've hit a ceiling vs. knowing you can still reach new heights."[2] Ageism is alive and well, but I for one am going to fight it all the way. Just by deciding to write this book at almost 60 years old, I'm fighting it and reaching new heights.

If you think you're too late, behind schedule, or that there's an age limit on success, think again. Some of the world's greatest thinkers, artists, writers, and inventors didn't find their groove until way later in life.

Famous painter Grandma Moses discovered her talent at 78; Frank McCourt wrote the Pulitzer Prize–winning memoir *Angela's Ashes* at 66; Laura Ingalls Wilder wrote the Little House on the Prairie series in her 60s; Colonel Sanders

2    Carol Dweck, *Mindset: The New Psychology of Success: How We Can Learn to Fulfill Our Potential* (New York: Ballantine, 2007).

founded Kentucky Fried Chicken at 65; and French Impressionist painter Paul Cézanne created his most valuable paintings at the end of his life.

Take that, child prodigies and overnight sensations!

## SOME OF US ARE JUST GETTING STARTED

Genius can strike young, but it's the post-50 kind of genius—the kind that strikes when you're older and wiser—that is the kind of genius that's most meaningful to me.

What this means is that you can be a badass at any age, and find your talent, potential, strength, purpose, and groove at any time. Even if you're not technically a late bloomer, there's always time to become who you really are or want to be. You will bloom. You will arrive. And as long as you keep marching, the beat will go on.

I believe we come into this world with a road map of who we'll become. There's destiny in how we grow up and evolve. Late bloomers in particular come with their own genetic road maps, but external factors count. It's the old nature vs. nurture question: Is human behavior and potential determined by environmental factors, or a person's genes? Is it inborn or learned? Or is it one's astrology? I know some of you will have no clue what I'm talking about here, but I have a Sun–Saturn conjunction in the first house, which portends a slow maturation process.

Whatever road map I had when I came into this world didn't make locating my destination any easier. I've gotten lost a million times, and could've used GPS. The problem is that life doesn't come with a directions app, so all you can hope for is a trusty internal compass or some good guidance along the way if you're lucky.

Some people follow a direct path; others, like me, take the scenic route, with twists and turns and a few unseen potholes. Like I said, nothing went according to plan for me, but as it turned out, it *was* the plan.

When late bloomers do arrive, it's nothing less than a miracle. Our struggle is real, but noted author and social observer Malcolm Gladwell has nothing but praise for our plight:

On the road to great achievement, the late bloomer will resemble a failure: while the late bloomer is revising and despairing and changing course and slashing canvases to ribbons after months or years, what he or she produces will look like the kind of thing produced by the artist who will never bloom at all. Prodigies are easy. They advertise their genius from the get-go. Late bloomers are hard. They require forbearance and blind faith. The Cézannes of the world bloom late not as a result of some defect in character, or distraction, or lack of ambition, but because the kind of creativity that proceeds through trial and error necessarily takes a long time to come to fruition.[3]

So don't count us late bloomers out. We may be late, but we're just getting started.

# TEST-DRIVEN TAKEAWAYS

There are 553,000 listings on Google for "Late-Bloomer Tips," and I can say with a fair amount of certainty, I've test-driven them all. The following are a few of my faves, with a few of my own thrown in:

- Throw out society's expectations and standards and create your own.
- Live, work, date, and love with intention and purpose.
- Own your own timeline and don't make apologies for it.
- Keep your eye on your own life, and don't compare it to others.
- Be prepared to reinvent a few times because you will.
- Quiet the noise in your head and breathe.

---

3    Malcolm Gladwell, "Late Bloomers: Why Do We Equate Genius with Precocity?," *The New Yorker*, October 13, 2008.

# LATE BLOOMER OR
# LOVEABLE FUCKUP?

*To be old and wise, you must first be young and stupid.*

—Unknown

You can't be a late bloomer without experiencing a few fuckups along the way.

Whether it's failing or falling on your face, fuckups can be beautiful stepping-stones to becoming your best self. Each try, each attempt, each effort—successful or not—gets you closer to being who you aspire to be.

Style icon and self-described geriatric starlet Iris Apfel says, "It takes time and effort to know who you are." It took her 99 years to figure that out. Her unique signature look (oversized round black glasses, stylishly cropped gray hair, and over-the-top costume jewelry) probably took that long to perfect.

Late bloomers, I have some good news for you: Failure can lead to big things.

I play a lot of online Scrabble and have amassed quite a few "bingos" in my day (using all seven tiles for one word, which is a big thing), but one bingo in particular stands out as one of my finest because it became my highest and most profound word score ever. I spelled out the word F-A-I-L-I-N-G-S by using all seven tiles and covering two triple point squares at the same time, which earned me a whopping 149 points.

The moral of this story is that I got my highest score with *failings*, an irony that wasn't lost on me. Seeing the word "failings" on the Scrabble board wasn't just an inside joke, it was affirmation that my fuckups weren't for nothing. True, they may have cost me at times and set me back, but the insight I got from my fuckups more than paid off. It's been said that the consolation prize of failure is what you've learned. I can vouch for this. What you learn from failure is like getting a Scrabble bingo.

I wrote a blog post a few years ago called "The Beauty of F\*\*king Up" to coincide with Yom Kippur, the Jewish Day of Atonement. I wrote it as a way of looking at atonement differently, which included my former self making amends to my current self. In the post I made the case for daily redemption, not just on one day a year, because every day is a chance to start over and do it better:

> On Yom Kippur, we're given a day to atone for our sins, to clean the slate, to clear our conscience, and make things right, while we fast for 24 hours as punishment for the past year's misdeeds. And when it's all over, we go back to our flawed selves, burying our shame and wrongdoings, until we bring them out again next year for reflection and redemption. I say atone it, own it, and be done with it. Not just for one day, but for *life*. That way you can be truly free.

Looking back, my former self did things I regret. It impeded my progress and undermined my success. It made bad choices and squandered opportunities. It had lapses in judgment, blew up perfectly good relationships, overreacted, or even worse, didn't act at all when it should have. Like the time I got an offer to be Roger Daltrey's trainer and go on tour with The Who. I stupidly turned it down because I didn't want to leave my boyfriend back at home, whom I ended up dumping a few weeks later anyway.

My former self also didn't handle money well, which leads me to confess another fuckup: If I knew I was going to be single for as long as I was, I would've started saving earlier or invested better. My thinking was, "I'm going to get married eventually, so why save? Why invest?"

Wrong! Why didn't someone tell me to stop buying shoes and start buying shares? Oh right, my parents did, and I didn't listen. Another fuckup!

## AS IF FUCKING UP WASN'T BAD ENOUGH

There's the shame, guilt, and regret that come after.

Shame, guilt, and regret can haunt you, even cripple you. They can prevent you from leaving the past behind and moving forward. Invite rumination to the party, and now your shame, guilt, and regret are raging on auto-repeat. That's because rumination takes your mistakes and replays them over and over on an endless loop in your head. I say this without shame when I tell you I'm still guilty of ruminating.

Arthur C. Brooks, host of the podcast *The Art of Happiness with Arthur Brooks*, explains rumination best:

> Rumination is to be stuck; self-reflection is to seek to be unstuck. The trick, of course, is telling the difference. Say you have just experienced a breakup. If you go over the painful circumstances again and again, like watching a looped video for hours and days, this is rumination. To break out of the cycle and begin the process of self-reflection, you'd have to follow the painful memory with insightful questions. For example: "Is this a recurring pattern in my life? If so, why?" "If I could do it over again, what would I do differently?" "What can I read to help inform me more about what I have just experienced and use it constructively?"[4]

---

4    Arthur C. Brooks, "Don't Wish for Happiness. Work for It," *The Atlantic*, April 22, 2021, https://www.theatlantic.com/family/archive/2021/04/working-wishing-happiness/618664/.

Using self-reflection as Arthur C. Brooks suggests makes me see my part clearly. It forces me to take responsibility, and action to correct it.

If you're having never-ending problems with friends or repeated disappointments in love, now would be a good time to understand what part you play in the whole dynamic.

Asking "What's my part?" is a mic drop moment. It's brave and bold. Not many people have the guts to ask, let alone consider what their part is, because it's too painful. Not many people can call themselves out because that would require honest self-reflection, accountability, and maybe even accepting blame. Oh, the horrors!

Self-reflection isn't for pussies. No one said it would be easy.

If there's any upside to shame, guilt, and regret, it's that they all make excellent drivers for self-improvement. They drive you to be better and do better, and self-reflection is the engine that powers it all.

## Bloom Like a Pro

As you bloom into the best version of yourself, don't take shame, guilt, and regret with you. Get rid of them now using these tips:

- Be in the present, stay in the present. Try not to go back, replay, or review.
- Turn self-punishment into self-compassion.
- Whatever mistake you made, remember you're not that person anymore. You might have been young, stupid, broke, or insecure—and now you're not.
- Find some humor in your circumstances and laugh off as much as you can.
- Make sure the love you have for yourself is bigger than the shame you carry.

## LET'S TALK ABOUT FORGIVENESS

Forgiveness is shame's worst enemy, and fucking up's best friend. Forgiveness will unburden, unblock, and set you free. When you fuck up (and you will, if you haven't already a million times) don't make things worse by beating yourself up with prolonged shame, regret, and rumination. Forgive yourself, early and often.

Now let's talk about forgiving others—the hardest thing you'll ever do, and the most loving gesture you can ever give yourself. Forgiving someone who wronged you isn't about letting them off the hook; it's about releasing the pain you carry because of them. When you forgive, you put yourself first and make your well-being a priority.

Practicing forgiveness has been like removing huge boulders of resentment that block my path. I say "practice" because like self-reflection, it takes work.

You may never get the apologies you think you're owed; you may never get the mea culpas you think you deserve; you may never get the "I'm sorry" you so desperately want to hear—so it's incumbent upon you to find your own forgiveness. Holding on to anger just gives your oppressor more power.

Most of my fuckups were self-inflicted, but as mentioned, there were times where I unintentionally caused pain to someone. As you can tell, I'm a big fan of making amends. I have no problem falling on my sword; I try to make things right, and when I say "I'm sorry" I mean it.

Sometimes forgiveness and grace work their magic, and you find your way back to someone. Sometimes it doesn't, and you lose them forever. If someone won't forgive you, then it's on you to find a way to forgive yourself.

I've been on all sides of the forgiveness equation, and here's what English poet Alexander Pope and I can tell you: "To err is human, to forgive, divine." If you can accept your failings and forgive yourself (and others), you're more than divine—you're my hero.

## DON'T WASTE A PERFECTLY GOOD FUCKUP

Erring comes with the territory for late bloomers. We fail and fall so many times, but we get back up and keep going. Trial and error, live and learn: You know the drill. You never want to waste a perfectly good fuckup by not learning from it.

Getting the lesson sometimes takes time, and as I've said, time is a bitch for late bloomers. We're either cursing it to go faster or wishing we could go back in time and do it over, but we can't. The only thing we can do is take the wisdom we got from our F-A-I-L-I-N-G-S and make a Scrabble bingo with it.

It's easy to confuse late starts for failure. It's easy to beat ourselves up because we didn't accomplish things within a certain time period. The reality is that some things in life just can't happen any sooner, like growing up, meeting your soulmate, or finding your calling. Do I wish I had gotten an earlier start to things? Sure. Do I wish I had my shit together in my 20s, even in my 30s and 40s? Of course. But if I had, I wouldn't have this story to tell.

# TEST-DRIVEN TAKEAWAY

Since the trainer in me puts everything into fitness terms, I've turned forgiveness into an exercise you can do anytime you're hurt or wronged.

First, start by seeing the perpetrator in your mind's eye not as an ugly ogre, but as a flawed, deeply unhappy person who might be in pain and suffering. When you consider the source of their pain, their childhood trauma, or the difficulties of their current circumstances, your anger will slowly turn to pity. Instead of feeling anger toward them, feel sorry for them. Doing this, your resentment turns to forgiveness, your heart softens, and you're transported to a more loving place. When you understand the source of someone's hurt, it won't hurt you as much.

# A NATURAL-BORN
# LATE BLOOMER

*The flower born into adversity is the most
beautiful and rare of all.*

—the Emperor to Mulan, in *Mulan*

You'd think my parents, Paul and Sonjia Brandon, would've gotten a clue I was going to be a late bloomer when I arrived on February 9, 1963, a full month after my due date. It was a sure sign I'd be taking my time.

There were other signs, too. When all my friends were buying bras, wearing makeup, and experimenting sexually, I was flat as a board, wearing tube socks, and skateboarding around my hometown of Beverly Hills. Nothing about me was in a hurry.

In high school and college I had crushes and fell madly in love, but long-term commitment was never my strong suit.

And it wasn't because I was emotionally scarred at a young age, although my first rejection was pretty traumatizing and could've deterred me from ever falling in love again. I was in 11th grade at Beverly Hills High, and the object of my affections was a cute senior three-sport stud with an early-1970s Bruce Jenner kind of look. We were on the track team together, sort of "dating," hardly in a relationship. Even so, he ended up dumping me for a freshman high-jumper. I was devastated, but more incensed that he left me for a younger woman.

To make matters worse, his mother was my English teacher, so even if I'd wanted to go full Glenn Close in *Fatal Attraction* on him (which I would never do), I couldn't, lest she give me a bad grade.

Other than three-sport stud who broke my heart (bruised my ego is more like it), most of my young relationships were trauma-free and full of discovery and wonder. My first real high school relationship came in the form of a varsity baseball player who came to Beverly his senior year. We took an immediate liking to each other, dated until he graduated, and on and off well into college and after. He was a great first boyfriend, and I've remained close to him and his family all these years.

As my relationship patterns started emerging and it became clear I wasn't a long-termer, my parents patiently endured every short-term boyfriend and held their tongues. But as their relationship patterns started emerging and it became clear they weren't normal, I didn't hold my tongue. I let them know how dysfunctional they were.

## GOOD-LOOKING BUT NUTS

My dad, with matinee idol good looks, was from Brooklyn. His mother was Jewish, his father was Italian, and my father was their only child. Interfaith marriage was unheard of back then, and it proved to be unsustainable. After his parents divorced there were contentious custody issues between the Italian side and his mother's Jewish side, so my father was sent away to an all-boys military school to avoid the tumult. This unfortunately caused a lifetime of trauma, abandonment, and bad memories for him. My father was a loving man and a nurturing father, but a tortured soul, I believe because of his childhood.

My movie-star beautiful mom was born in Northern Ireland, raised in Scotland, and came to America in her early 20s. One of her first jobs was a secretary at CBS, where she worked for some of TV's early greats, including Rod Serling of *The Twilight Zone*. My father was a young literary agent at William Morris at the same time, and when they met during a writers strike in the late 1950s, it was love at first sight. They were married for 10 years.

My parents are good people, but not exactly role models for healthy relationships. To me, a healthy relationship is a mutually nurturing, stable, and committed partnership. I never saw that. I saw two people who had great love for each other but, for many reasons, couldn't make it work. As a result, I grew up thinking love was inherently painful and angst-ridden. My mother eventually asked for a divorce, and Dad reluctantly agreed. I was seven at the time. Shortly after they split, my father moved out, my mother went to work, and I officially became a latchkey child.

The dysfunction was, even though they divorced, they never really split.

They couldn't let go; they couldn't quite disconnect, and they never truly detached. They stayed enmeshed in every aspect of each other's lives, business, and health for years after their marriage. This was never more the case than when my mother was diagnosed with Type 1 diabetes at 60. Even though my parents were long divorced, my father still launched into action like a good husband, taking her to every doctor's appointment and tending to her every need.

Even when they were dating other people (or trying to, as was more the case) they felt guilty and conflicted. You might think this was romantic; it wasn't. As their go-between, they told me too much, I knew too much, saw too much, and too often was sucked into their drama. Their relationship was as codependent as you could get, and I was smack in the middle of it.

My childhood was totally DIY: find your own way and figure it out yourself. My parents were working full time in Hollywood; Dad started his own literary agency after William Morris, and Mom had opened her own commercial talent agency, Commercials Unlimited, a major milestone for a female at the time. They were busy building their businesses and figuring out single parenthood, while I had to find structure wherever I could, mostly by creating it myself. As loved and cared for as I was, I had to self-parent a lot of the time.

Growing up in Beverly Hills, I went to school with the offspring of famous people, socialized with my parents' celebrity circle, and pretty much experienced the whole groovy entertainment scene from my living room—which wasn't in a huge mansion with butlers (like some of my friends) but in a chic Beverly Hills apartment "below the tracks," as they used to say, when a railroad ran through Beverly Hills, back in the day. My parents were at the epicenter of hip, mixing it up with movers and shakers of all kinds. Think *Real Housewives of Beverly Hills*, minus the backstabbing and Botox.

Even though my father was a "Sunday Dad" (back then, divorced dads only had Sundays, no shared custody or alternating living arrangements), he was very much a part of my life. He was an extremely devoted, hands-on father who taught me how to ride a bike, drive a car, hit a tennis ball, and wager on sports. When I was little, I'd sit at his knee watching football, and he'd teach me everything about the game, and how to bet on it.

Despite my dad's sports betting obsession, he was a very cerebral man who turned me on to the philosophical writings of Ralph Waldo Emerson when I was 12, Max Ehrmann's famous prose poem "Desiderata" when I was 16, and played the music of jazz greats Stan Getz, Antonio Carlos Jobim, Ella Fitzgerald, and Sergio Mendes from the time I can remember.

Paul Brandon was a cool cat. He wore beads in the 1970s, smoked weed, slept on a waterbed, had a black light in his refrigerator, and named me "Treva" at a time when there were mostly Jills and Debbies. He even put my name on his license plate—TREVAB.

After the divorce, we developed our own special Daddy–Daughter relationship. We had our own language, handshake, and nicknames. He called me "Youngblood," "Chalk Chick" ("Chalk" is a betting term for "favorite"), and "Alpha Chick," a nod to the strong little girl he raised. He gave himself the nickname "Captain Groovy," which all my school friends called him—and still do.

We even had our own special 11th Commandment between us: "Thou shalt not lie to or put on thy father."

As evolved as my father was, he was emotionally very broken, as I noted, and the divorce only made it worse. My mother, for good measure, had her own brand of nuts, stemming from a long-running narrative that she was unwanted as a child because she was the last one born into a family of six girls, and didn't get the love she needed. She harbored a deep resentment of her mother for this, and of course, I had to hear about it because you know, TMI.

**Both of my parents had unhealed wounds, both were nuts, and both couldn't figure out if they were coming or going, which made me nuts.**

Both of my parents had unhealed wounds, both were nuts, and both couldn't figure out if they were coming or going, which made me nuts. In modern dating terms, it's called "trauma bonding." And I truly believe it was what kept them together.

## PARENTING MY PARENTS

Not only did my parents not handle their baggage very well, they handed it down to me. Clinically defined as "generational trauma," my parents' trauma became my trauma, and our family dynamic. It was the gift that unfortunately kept on giving as I grew up.

On many of our Sundays my father and I would end up sitting on the beach or the Santa Monica pier—and he'd start to cry. It was always over the divorce, or my mother, the loss of our little family unit, or remembering his own painful childhood. I'd put my arms over his shoulder and do my best to comfort him. "Don't worry, Daddy," I'd say, "everything's going to be all right."

I was probably eight or nine years old at the time and had no idea that everything was going to be all right. In fact, I was scared to death everything was *not* going to be all right and seeing him so fragile scared me even more. Nonetheless, I did my best to reassure him that even though the marriage had failed, I would be OK. As a result of watching my father, I grew up thinking love is tortured, and all men need healing.

In many ways helping my parents sort out their troubles was some of my earliest life coaching work. They were my first clients, so to speak, and not very good ones.

In trying to understand their needs, I came to understand my own. Maybe it was the times or their generation, but their style of parenting was fly-by-the-seat-of-your-pants—very different from today's helicopter moms and dads. I loved the spontaneity and freedom, but craved stability. As a result, I developed an excessive need for control because I felt I had so little of it.

I recently reconnected with one of my old nannies, and when I asked her what I was like back then, she said I was a "compliant kid." I didn't make trouble, probably because I didn't want the extra chaos that came with it. I had enough already.

Because my parents weren't always around and because I was alone so much, I had to become my own little pillar of strength. I discovered back then that emotional strength and self-reliance were my most precious natural resources, and they still are as an adult. Early on I learned to rely on myself, cope with my emotions, and be my own best friend. (Which would turn out to be great training for single life.) And whatever I couldn't handle, I'd turn to my extended family for help (my grandmother might've been horrible, but at least she had the good sense to give me nine first cousins who were like brothers and sisters to me).

As I said, my parents definitely paved the way for my future as a life coach. I wish I could say my early work with them was successful, but unfortunately, they were unfixable. Not that it was my job in the first place to fix them, but I took it on, and they didn't exactly refuse my services.

Unlike my father, my mother, Sonjia, moved on pretty quickly after the divorce, by throwing herself into the agency business. She was the original 1970s liberated woman, an accidental feminist, the original girl boss, and the inspiration for my independent spirit. Both parents gave me my work ethic, but my mother was the day-to-day embodiment of it.

Commercials Unlimited and my mother grew to great heights. From a two-room office to a commercial talent powerhouse, Sonjia represented thousands of actors, booked thousands of jobs, and made a lot of money doing it. She was a savvy negotiator, whether it was for a scale actor or a celebrity endorsement. Her clients loved her, and even more impressive, stayed with her, despite the fickle nature of the entertainment industry. Like Tim Allen, whom she's represented for over 30 years, who continues to be a good friend and loyal client. I had a front-row seat to her ascendance because I was either hanging out at her office after school or seeing her bring her work home after a long day at the office. The job never stopped, and neither did she.

She was so successful, in fact, that she never took a penny from my father. This immigrant from Northern Ireland, with only a high school diploma, had become the American Dream, and she is regarded as an icon in the industry to this day.

As inspiring a woman as my mother was in the working world, she was less so in the traditional sense of being a woman or mom, which didn't include PTA meetings or baking cookies. Domestic goddess wasn't her aspiration.

Her true calling was to be the president of her own company, not a house-wife. She was ambitious, not domestic; she'd rather make deals than make dinner. I like to say she was married to her business, and that "marriage" with Commercials Unlimited lasted 45 years.

When it came to me and boys, there wasn't a lot of mother–daughter guid-ance. I was left to my own devices to figure out the facts of life, entrusting one of my childhood best friends, Kim, instead of my mother, to teach me how to use a tampon when I finally got my period at almost 15.

## DATING TIPS FROM THE WOMAN WHO HARDLY DATED

When it came to dating, though, my mother did lead by example. Her personal life was never a revolving door of men, probably because she was too busy building her agency. In the 50 years since her divorce she's only had two boyfriends. Work consumed her, defined her, and gave her validation like no relationship could.

She was my first glimpse of a strong, independent woman and role model for what I could achieve in life. As a single mom and businesswoman, she taught me lessons like "Don't go out of the house without lipstick," and "Whenever you're negotiating, don't throw out the first number." She was old-school glam, always wearing heels and makeup, and she was old-school practical when she'd chastise me for not carrying cash with me at all times.

Sonjia is all work, but all play too. She knows how to have fun. She has a wild side that curses like a sailor and drinks like a fish. She loves to throw parties, go on cruises with her sisters, and compete in slots tournaments in Vegas. She's a high-roller and a big tipper. She loves to dance. After we bought the *Saturday Night Fever* 8-track back in 1978, we did the hustle in our living room for an entire year.

She is elegance, class, and style personified. She rocked hip huggers and midriffs in the 1970s just as hard as she's rocked Chanel in her later years as an agent. She was driven and ambitious, but thoroughly feminine. All curves, no hard edges.

As beautiful as my mother is, she's equally as funny. Her sense of humor is world-class. She has a sharp wit, is quick with the puns, and is a sucker for a good Henny Youngman one-liner. For example, if we ever checked into a hotel and the room was small, the first thing out of her mouth was: "I wouldn't say our room was small, but the mice are hunchbacked." Or "I wouldn't say our room was small, but when you put the key in the door, you broke the window." Her sense of humor was so disarming you'd look at her and wonder how someone so beautiful could also be so funny.

What's even funnier is that this same woman who used to tell me to wear lipstick and not throw out the first number in a negotiation would also say: "Don't be so funny, you'll scare men away."

Of all her unique qualities, I'd say her most defining was that she never seemed to need a man. She never pursued, she never initiated. While I may have had lapses in judgment when it came to guys, the one thing I never did was chase one, which was a big no-no in her book. My mother was never showy, needy, or clingy—and I took note. In her worldview men pursue you, not the other way around. It's old fashioned, especially in today's women-make-the-first-move dating app world, but it was her personal code and mine too, to an extent. It has on more than one occasion stopped me from making myself too available or too desperate.

## SPORTS AND SINGLEHOOD

As I outgrew nannies and babysitters, my survival skills and self-sufficiency kicked in. I learned to make my own breakfast, do my own laundry, and ride the two-mile trek to school on my bike without a helmet. I was a privileged Beverly Hills Jewish girl, though hardly a princess. Once I hit high school, I was a typical teenager who loved clothes, boys, and hanging out, but was also a serious athlete who found structure through sports.

Being an athlete taught me discipline, mental toughness, pushing through pain, and never quitting. My race was the 400 meters—not for sissies—and I took it on and toughed it out, as I did with most things in life.

Just as growing up an only child prepared me well for singlehood, so did sports, which I have found often requires the same stamina and endurance. My athletic background also came in handy when I got a job as a group fitness instructor in college, which coincided with the early days of Jane Fonda and the aerobics craze. It was a perfect fit: me in leg warmers, barking out orders, corralling a class with choreographed kicks and crunches. Teaching fitness classes would become a constant for me, regardless of where I lived or was working.

**Just as growing up an only child prepared me well for singlehood, so did sports, which I have found often requires the same stamina and endurance.**

The fitness bug also bit my mother, who became a full-fledged gym rat when I was in high school. She turned into a competitive runner and "sports mom," who attended every one of my track meets and volleyball games.

In academics, I was a late bloomer too. I graduated from high school with an average GPA, but eventually channeled my inner brainiac and became a full-fledged smarty-pants once I hit college. I loved school, but I was a restless soul and ended up going to three different colleges in four years (Santa Barbara, City College, the University of Colorado in Boulder, and UC Santa Barbara), and despite always being late, somehow I managed to graduate on time with a BA in Liberal Studies.

I was convinced the commitment-phobe gene was hereditary until my father finally remarried at 69 and proved me wrong. It was a feat I thought I'd never see in my lifetime. Because there was always so much hesitancy about letting go, you can imagine my sigh of relief when he finally did, and tied the knot with a new wife.

The only thing I'd ever wanted for both parents was to find peace and happiness, even if it was with other spouses. So when actress and dancer Suzanne

Charny, of 1960s and 1970s TV and movie fame, came into our lives along with her daughter Stacy, I welcomed them both with open arms. I finally had a sister, and my father finally had a wife who would heal his heart and help him move on.

I breathed another sigh of relief that my parents' long-suffering drama would come to a close, or at least I thought. But on the day of my father's wedding, I made a visit to my mom's, and overheard her belting out Gloria Gaynor's "I Will Survive" to the radio. It was at this moment I realized their drama wasn't coming to a close anytime soon because she couldn't handle not having him. She loved him deeply, but she also loved being loved by him. She got used to his attention and affections and didn't want them to end. Today we would see this as narcissistic, but back then, it was standard operating procedure for my parents.

I watched her melodramatics and said, "Oh please. You'll survive. We'll all survive. Get over it already."

I was 36 at the time, and my peace and happiness were all over the map. I wasn't even close to getting serious about my own future marriage prospects, and definitely not anywhere near a husband or a chuppa. I had no idea what it took to get married or stay married, because of course when it came to love and relationships, I was raised by wolves.

It would take many more years to figure it out, and by "figure it out," I mean determining whether I was even the marrying type to begin with.

# THE LATE BLOOMER GETS DEFLOWERED

*It's not too late at all.*
*You just don't know what you're capable of.*

—Gandhi

**T**he fact that I lost my virginity at almost 22 should actually give you fewer clues about me as a late bloomer and more about me as a control freak (there's that Virgo moon again).

It wasn't for religious reasons, or because I was a prude, or had weird sexual hang-ups or trust issues. I was just in no hurry to give it up, plain and simple. Don't get me wrong: I had my fair share of fooling around in my teenage years, I just always stopped short of going all the way.

The reason why I held out for so long was because I had some strange, romantic notion that losing your virginity should be a special, sacred moment that shouldn't be given to just anyone, so I kept waiting for some perfect situation, but the situations were never perfect enough.

The choice to stay a virgin was all mine, and I liked it that way. I liked having complete control—over my body, boys, and destiny. Control gave me agency to set my own terms and conditions. Thankfully, the guys in high school and college were patient and understood this to be the only way to get in my pants. They never pressured me, never issued ultimatums or made me feel bad.

But after so many hand jobs, a girl had to wonder: Is that all there is? I started rethinking my virginity—maybe it wasn't so precious after all. Maybe it was time to see what all the fuss was about. Maybe my control issues were a hindrance, not a protective device. Maybe they were holding me back when I should be giving it up.

## AND NOW, THE MOMENT
## WE'VE ALL BEEN WAITING FOR

That all changed during a summer session at Harvard University between my junior and senior year of college. I was studying there with my roommate Karen from UC Santa Barbara, and it was on one hot, rainy Boston day in between classes that I decided to do the deed with a fellow student named Paul from North Carolina, a guy I had been dating that summer. He was tall, skinny, shy, and kind of geeky, but most of all he was a gentleman, so I decided to give him the honors. Even though he was a perfectly lovely guy, it wasn't love; it was a necessity, as I was fed up with waiting for the perfect person or moment. At the rate I was going, no one would be good enough.

As horny college kids are wont to do, we found ourselves in his dorm room making out before class when the idea came to me. I liked him, felt comfortable enough, and wasn't getting any younger, so I made him an offer he couldn't refuse.

The following transaction was all business, hardly romantic, and exactly how it went down (no pun intended).

ME: I have a crazy question. Would you have sex with me?

His eyes widen, unsure if I'm joking.

I sit up on his bed, straighten myself, adjust my ponytail, and look him directly in the eye.

ME: I've been waiting forever, and it's getting ridiculous. I kind of want to get it over with already.

I look at my watch. Time is ticking, not because I've been waiting forever but because I have class in an hour, so we have to hurry. He looks confused, but doesn't ask questions. I go into negotiation mode.

ME: There are some ground rules. First, you need to go super slow, OK?

He nods, maybe gulps, I can't remember.

ME: Then I want you to let me know where you are every inch of the way.

I say this without any hint of irony or humor. This devirginizing is serious.

ME: Oh, and one more thing: *no thrusting*. I want you to go in and get out, OK?

I use hand signals in case he doesn't get the point. He nods again.

ME: Oh, and no coming either. Got it?

HIM: Yes, I think I've got it.

The deal is done, and we get to work, with rules and restrictions in place. With our clothes partially removed, the Devirginizer is doing exactly what I asked: not thrusting, hardly moving. I'm definitely not enjoying it, and he isn't either.

ME: Are you in yet?

HIM: Almost.

A minute or two passes, and it's not getting any better. He's struggling, and I'm not feeling anything remotely orgasmic. I'm rolling my eyes, thinking to myself, *Never has one waited so long for so little. This thing they call "fucking" is totally overrated.*

HIM: OK, I think I'm in.

ME: Are you sure?

HIM: Yep.

No magical moment, no theatrical climax, no fireworks. He stops moving, exactly per my orders. He also doesn't come, also per my orders. Besides, he's way too proper to shoot his load without asking permission first.

I can't remember if I thanked him or hugged him. All I remember is that our parting was sweet but business-like, as I had to hurry off to class. But first, I ran to the public phone bank at the Harvard library to share the good news with my father. He was so thrilled upon hearing it that he sent me a dozen roses the next day with a card that said: "Now you're really a communications major!" Right after his call I called my mom, who promptly chewed me out for not using birth control.

My devirginization wasn't very romantic, nor was it the least bit sacred, but it was special in its own way and very predictive of how I would handle future romantic encounters. The Devirginizer got the job done, and I finally got over the hump, as it were.

Postscript: after summer session ended at Harvard and before heading back to UC Santa Barbara for our senior year, my roommate Karen and I ventured to Nantucket for a few days with the Devirginizer in tow. He had friends there with a guest room, so we came along for the ride, hoping for free accommodations. But once we got there Karen and I ditched him, and proceeded to embark on a Girls Gone Wild weekend. It wouldn't last long, though, because Karen ended up meeting a guy in a local Nantucket bar two days into our stay, which put a different spin on our single girl adventure. She ended up marrying him a few years later when she was 24, and went on to have three beautiful children—while I, on the other hand, continued to be a girl gone wild for another 27 years.

When I mentioned earlier that life never went according to plan for me, I wasn't kidding. While I was getting deflowered, all my friends were getting engaged. When they were getting married and setting up house, I was their bridesmaid living in an apartment. When they were having children, I was still having boy problems. When they were suffering with unruly teenagers, I was suffering with aging parents who behaved like unruly teenagers. When my friends were getting divorced, I was settling down. When they were looking at colleges for their kids, I was looking at wedding venues.

When they were getting colonoscopies at 50, I was getting married.

## WAITING FOR THE HIGH HARD ONE

I may have been an old virgin, but I'm far from the oldest. A journalist named Amanda McCracken has me beat. She's the real Late-Blooming Virgin.

She wrote a very personal and moving *Huffington Post* article titled "I Waited Until I Was 41 To Lose My Virginity."[5] The writer reminded me a lot of myself—not in that we both waited to have sex, but that we both waited for something more meaningful. I waited till I was 51 for marriage; she waited till she was 41 to get the high hard one. Upon reflection, she said: "My extended journey as a virgin made me discover things about myself I might have never realized had I had sex with the first guy who insisted. Ultimately, it took a lot of time, as well as awareness and work to stop my self-destructive patterns and allow myself to be loved."

If I replaced "sex" with "marriage," this could easily be my story. Amanda McCracken waited to have sex because she didn't want to get hurt. I waited to get married because I didn't know myself, and to know myself would take work and time. Her decision was based on self-protection, while mine was self-exploration.

Looking back on our choice to wait, we both ask ourselves: Was it worth it? We both emphatically say yes. Like Amanda, my extended journey as a late life first-time bride made me discover things about myself I might have never realized had I gotten married sooner. Plus, waiting for the right person made it all worth it.

Spoiler alert: Amanda eventually fell in love, lost her virginity, and married a man who made her feel safe and loved. As she ends her story, she admits that it wasn't really about sex, or waiting for the perfect guy to show up. It was about "Waiting on a healthy me to show up, the one who realized she deserved more than breadcrumbs."

Same here. I also waited on a healthy me to show up, but I waited for a healthy partner to show up, too.

There are those who find their person, get married, and have babies in their 20s; those who are established professionally by their 30s; those who have it all by 40; and those who at 50, are already planning for their golden years. And

---

5   Amanda McCracken, "I Waited Until I Was 41 to Lose My Virginity. But Was It Worth It?," *Huffington Post*, February 14, 2020, https://www.huffpost.com/entry/losing-virginity-41-virgin-shelf-life_n_5e419ffcc5b6f1f57f16b014.

then there are those like me, maybe like you, who need a bit more time, maybe a little more faith, too.

Faith isn't my strong suit, and it only became harder to find the older I got. Life wasn't happening to me like it was for my friends. Their achievements seemed to pass me up. Not keeping up, not fitting in, and being left behind only reinforced my feelings of inadequacy and hopelessness. It was easy to lose faith.

As I've come to learn, we don't need to have it all figured out by a certain age. There's no date to be married by, or deadline for achievement. Just because you don't hit your benchmarks in a timely fashion—or hit them at all—doesn't make you a failure; it just makes you *you*.

It's only natural to want to hurry up and get there; we're all impatient when we want something, and it's not even a late-bloomer thing. But ask author and professor Savala Nolan, and she'll tell you not to be in such a rush. In her essay "On Slowness," Nolan not only illustrates the beauty of taking your time, she also uses a flower metaphor to do it (which is so my brand!):

> How my roses and alyssum cannot be forced to bloom, they just have to be cared for with patience and consideration. It's good medicine. It's an antidote to the algorithmic insanity of the cultural moment. To know how to wait and stay grounded is, I think, part of living well. To wait with appreciation for the process, and to tend to the process with appreciation. That's a gift to ourselves, and to others. Let the good times roll, yes, and also let them be still, let them come slowly, the longer we might savor them.[6]

I'm no Zen master (or horticulturist), but I'm pretty sure everything blooms when it's supposed to and works out the way it should—from when you give

6    Savala Nolan, "On Slowness," *Human Parts*, May 27, 2022, https://humanparts.medium.com/
     on-slowness-8e71d20cfdf6.

up the goods to when you tie the knot. The best thing you can do is enjoy the ride—even if it takes forever.

# TEST-DRIVEN TAKEAWAY

In his book *Late Bloomers: The Power of Patience in a World Obsessed with Early Achievement*, author and *Forbes* magazine editor Rich Karlgaard reminds us that "In every aspect of our lives, there are many, equally valid ways to reach a positive outcome. There are always many ways to achieve a goal, gain expertise, or find success."[7]

I'm test-driven proof of this. So are those who've opted to take the scenic route instead of the road most-traveled. If your journey is to achieve a goal, gain expertise, find success, love, purpose, or your place in the world, it's your call on how to get there. Take an unconventional route, an alternative path, the express lane, or the slow boat to China—you've got my blessings. Go get your positive outcome any way you can get it.

---

7    Rich Karlgaard, *Late Bloomers: The Power of Patience in a World Obsessed with Early Achievement* (Penguin Random House, April 2019), https://www.latebloomer.com.

# THE LATE BLOOMER FINDS
# HERSELF BY ACCIDENT

*Not till we are completely lost or turned around,*
*do we begin to find ourselves.*

—Henry David Thoreau

From boyfriend to breakup and breakup to boyfriend, romance was a series of starts and stops for me. Not that I didn't meet great guys; I did, especially in my mid-30s, when I was in my prime. I had good taste and dated solid dudes, some I even brought home to mother. I had boyfriends I loved and who loved me, and any number of them would've probably married me—but no one asked, because I couldn't get that far.

I was a runaway girlfriend.

This of course made my mother crazy. Once I broke up with a perfectly nice boyfriend on whom she was counting to be her son-in-law, and she thought I had lost my mind. On paper he was Mr. Right, and yet, I couldn't do it. She must've asked me a million times why I wanted to end it, and a million times I couldn't come up with an answer other than "I'm not ready."

The truth was, I didn't want to settle—or rather, I didn't know how. The only thing I knew was that marriage, at that time, wasn't right for me, and to do it any sooner, or with the wrong person, would be settling. I had to be true to myself.

My mother managed well without a man but didn't want me following in her footsteps. It was "Do as I say, not as I do." The problem was, I was managing just as well without a man as she was, if not better. What I wasn't managing well was following in her professional footsteps.

In the early 1990s I took a break from advertising to work at her agency, trying it on for size, even though I'd grown up with it and already knew the drill. Booking actors, dealing with casting directors and ad agency executives, and traveling for commercial shoots, I tried to love being an agent like she did, but couldn't. Even traveling with Tim Allen on his commercial shoots—which was the most fun you could ever have—wasn't enough to make me want to switch careers.

I met some great people during my brief stint as an agent, one being Bill Maher. This was years before his HBO show, before he was a household name, when he was still a stand-up comedian. I thought he was super funny and told my mother she should sign him for commercials. At one point, he asked me out to dinner, and of course I went because I was already a fan.

He took me to a super hip restaurant in Hollywood, and before we got out of the car, we lit up a joint and took a few hits. Twenty minutes later, we were chatting at the table, and the topic of my relationship status came up. I guess I was more stoned than I thought, because when he asked why I was still single, I tried to say I was on a "dating hiatus," but I accidentally said *"hating diatus,"* which caused a minutes-long stoned laughing fit at the table. It's one of those "you had to be there" stories, but trust me when I tell you we were in hysterics. I honestly thought he was going to fall off his chair.

It might've been a Freudian slip, because the truth was, I really did hate the agency business. So after my dinner with Bill, I quit my mom, went back to free-lance copywriting, and freelancing romantically, too.

This of course meant more dates, more change, more searching, and more connecting for short periods of times, but never attaching. Yet in the summer of 1999, I met someone I thought could change all that.

## MR. ALMOST RIGHT

It was at a party, and Marvin Gaye's "Got to Give It Up" was playing as I arrived. I literally danced my way into the living room, and that's where he saw me. We made eye contact, and a connection was made.

Originally from Boulder, Colorado, but living in LA, my new connection was cute, funny, and an Aries, a fire sign compatible with mine. I liked him immediately. I gave him my number; a first date was planned, and soon after, a nickname was given: Aries Pig (a combination of Western astrology and Eastern astrology, since he was born in the Chinese year of the Pig). As I would soon find out, Aries Pig was freshly separated, a minor inconvenience that didn't deter me or him. His situation was fraught with challenges—not just because he was separated, but because he was also still living in the house with his soon-to-be ex. This made dating him problematic, but not impossible.

Six months into a deepening relationship, I actually could see myself marrying him. I was about to turn 40, and my latent commitment gene was finally making its long-awaited appearance.

But right in the middle of our romance, just as the ink was drying on his divorce papers and he was becoming more public with our relationship, he relocated back to Boulder. We did the long-distance thing for a while—every few weeks I was either flying to Boulder, or he was flying to LA. It went like this for almost two years, and somehow we managed to keep the relationship going. Even long distance he was a devoted boyfriend, but as with most separated or newly divorced guys, he still had healing to do and things to figure out. I came into his life too soon, and he was still enmeshed with his ex-wife.

I had seen this story before with my parents; I had seen what being enmeshed with your ex-wife looks like and I didn't want to repeat it, but I didn't know how to end it. But the universe ended up doing for me what I couldn't do myself.

After one of our typical visits in the summer of 2001, I was in the back of a town car going to Denver International Airport to fly home when I got into a near-death car accident on the freeway. It was no accident, though; it was the cosmic signal I needed that our relationship wasn't meant to be.

An 18-wheeler tractor trailer veered into our lane and slammed into us. Our car flipped over a freeway embankment and went airborne. As soon as we hit the ground, the force of the roof caved down on my head and broke my neck.

When the car came to rest upside down, my first instinct was to escape the car in case it exploded. In shock, and having no idea I was injured, I crawled out the shattered rear window and ran for my life down the grassy median of the freeway. Good Samaritans witnessed the collision, called an ambulance, and the driver and I were rushed to the hospital.

It was only after x-rays were taken that I found out I had fractured my cervical spine.

There was no dislocation or paralysis, but I still wasn't out of the woods. I spent the next week at Denver General Hospital with Aries Pig at my side. Eventually, I was put into a plastic and metal half-body brace and sent home. After three months living in the brace (even sleeping and bathing in it) and many more months of physical therapy afterward, I made a full and miraculous recovery. I still have some lingering range-of-motion issues and pain from time to time, but I'm not in a wheelchair, so I don't complain.

The accident proved to be a turning point. I survived and recovered, but the relationship didn't. There was no official breakup; we just knew it was over, and that was OK. He represented a significant moment in my life and for that reason, I always knew we'd stay in touch.

Ex-boyfriends, I've noticed, can serve as important markers for one's growth and progress. I can look back and remember certain times of my life by who I was dating. Those relationships may not have lasted, but each one would continue to inch me forward in my pursuit of love.

## I LOVE A GOOD EPIPHANY

There are two things that will change a person's life: a near-death experience, and the epiphany that comes after. My epiphany was overwhelming gratitude. Because of the accident I am thankful for every little thing, every little gesture, and for the outcome I was spared.

To this day, no matter how bad things get, I always remember the alternative

and quickly shut my mouth. There's nothing like surviving a near-death experience to make you stop whining.

The accident also became an unintentional reinvention for me. At the time I
was a copywriter and teaching fitness classes at Equinox and Barry's Bootcamp.
I never took the fitness business seriously, but then the accident happened, and
somehow fitness became a new career.

My segue into full-time fitness happened when a fellow instructor—who was
also a private trainer—asked me if I wanted to take over her client. I had never
worked one-on-one with anyone, it sounded interesting, so I said yes.

I started working with this client, and before long, I changed her body. She
got fit and defined, and I was like a proud artist who sculpted her. Soon word
got out among her friends and fellow school moms about her new trainer, and
suddenly I was in demand. Twenty years later, it's the longest gig I've ever had.

During this time I found another calling: volunteering. Since I didn't have
children of my own (but still held out hope I would one day), I chose the
Fulfillment Fund mentoring organization to lend my support and unharnessed
maternal instincts. The Fulfillment Fund matches adults with at-risk kids in
underserved communities. The emphasis is on education, and the goal is to
get your mentee through high school and on to college. You stay matched
with your mentee for four years, and during that time you teach them about
life, discipline, responsibility, and boys (my wheelhouse, of course). Because
I never had a mentor or big sister growing up, I knew the value of having a
strong guiding force in a young girl's life; I threw myself into the mission and
tried to shape as many destinies as I could, while my own destiny continued
to take shape.

## SHOW ME YOUR VULNERABILITY
## AND I'LL SHOW YOU YOUR STRENGTH

I also threw myself into being a trainer. I was making good money, working hard,
making my own hours, calling my own shots, never taking a day off. I worked
weekends, holidays, late nights, before sunrise, even with injuries and illnesses,
nonstop. I was always on-call and never said no.

I've trained clients of all shapes, sizes, ages, and abilities: celebrities, working moms, executives, retirees, even Middle Eastern royalty. I've turned an overweight single dad into the Six-Million Dollar Man, an 80-year-old grandma into the Bionic Woman, and a Qatari princess into an Olympic athlete.

I had some difficult clients too. Like the entitled Beverly Hills socialite, ex-wife of a British lord. When her kids destroyed a piece of equipment I left at her house, I politely asked if she was going to replace it. She became so incensed that I dared ask, she retorted back: "My ex-husband had a saying for people like you: 'Your breeding is showing.'"

After picking my jaw up off the floor after having my breeding questioned, I fired off an email the next day, reminding her that people with good "breeding" take responsibility and don't stiff their trainers.

Other than her, I loved my job and clients and took great pride in the impact I knew I was having on them. Over the years, many of them have become my dear friends—an unintended benefit of working so closely and developing trust with them. Of all my gigs, fitness was the most rewarding because I knew I was changing lives, not just bodies.

All my clients have stories and secrets, sometimes deep pain and fear. Some are afraid of losing their edge or their looks. Some are at the top of their game or staging their comeback. Some are ashamed of their bodies or afraid of failure. Some are former athletes and know their bodies, and some don't have an athletic bone in their body. All of them, though, have one thing in common: Once they hit the gym, they're all the same.

The gym is the great equalizer, and one of the few places (other than a therapist's couch) that make people feel vulnerable. I loved the vulnerability part; my clients avoided it at all costs. They wanted to feel as invincible as they did in the rest of their life, but invariably an exercise in our workout would make them feel foolish or weak and they'd refuse to do it. What they failed to understand, according to bestselling author Brené Brown, is that "Vulnerability is not weakness; it's our greatest measure of courage."[8] When you make yourself vulnerable, you automatically get stronger.

---

8    Brené Brown, *Rising Strong: The Reckoning. The Rumble. The Revolution* (New York: Random House, 2015).

The car accident that made me feel so vulnerable actually introduced me to my purpose and strength: to heal, empower, and show people their greatness, which in turn showed me my own greatness.

Whether I was training clients or teaching group exercise, I was 100% committed. Yet as committed to my career as I was, I still couldn't find someone to commit to me.

## THERE'S A DROUGHT IN MY POOL

I was 40, and the prospects weren't getting any better—in fact, they were getting worse.

Still, I kept myself out there, looking for dating opportunities everywhere I went, including the gym, which is a big dating no-no when you're a trainer.

I broke my own rule of not dating clients and once dated one. It ended horribly, and I ended up firing him, which cost me a good chunk of income. A couple years later he called to ask if I'd be willing to train him again, but this time it would be all business, no monkey business. I agreed, with this caveat: "I'm going to charge you a lot more and beat the shit out of you." He was up for it. Moral of the story: he was a lousy boyfriend, but a good client, and sometimes that's even better.

My career continued to flourish and grow, although I couldn't say the same for my dating life. Striking out IRL, I did what any smart, single person would do who was looking for love: I went online.

## TEST-DRIVEN TAKEAWAYS

Finding a new direction or reason to reinvent can come suddenly or subtly. My car accident was the catalyst for my reinvention, and though I don't wish a catastrophe or crisis upon anyone, it did change the course of my life. The fact is, you're never too old and it's never too late to reinvent, and there are countless ways to do it, according to my friend Kathi Sharpe-Ross, author of *Reinvent Your Life! What Are You Waiting For?*

Here are her Power Tools for reinvention.[9]

1. **Read the signs:** Actively listen to yourself—reflect and lean into it. Do not sweep those feelings under the rug or shrug off those thoughts. Be mindful of the gnawing feeling, the things you're questioning, and why you're questioning them, and allow this to be important to you. Evaluate the present. Don't ignore the signs—now's the time to be in control and manifest what you want and make it happen.

2. Understand the **pros and cons** of what you're facing. Take out a piece of paper, make columns, and start to truly identify the pros and cons to what you're contemplating. The greatest way to hold the truth up to yourself is by writing things down and giving your thoughts and feelings a voice.

3. Establish what you **value vs. your time**. Make a list of all that you deeply value in your life—and be truly honest. Now make a list of where and how you're actually spending your time. Then sit back and see where those two columns actually align. Odds are, they don't! Now it's time to reset your priorities and establish how you can bring these two columns into greater alignment.

4. **Create a plan** and move to **action**—take baby steps—break it down and focus on each piece, one at a time. Whether it's a five-minute reinvention or a 10-year reinvention, you are *entitled* to have what you want in life. With small risks come great rewards, so what are you waiting for?

5. Don't let your own past limitations, hurdles, or failures limit your expectations of what you are able to experience right here and now. What you expect, you experience. Sometimes when life breaks things apart, it allows us to rebuild ourselves—and our lives—even stronger. Try to see the opportunity in every life change, and you will undoubtedly find yourself on the most amazing—and unexpected—adventure.

---

9    Reported to me in May 2022.

# A PIONEER WOMAN IN THE
# WILD WEST OF LOVE

*Actually, the best gift you could have ever given*
*her was a lifetime of adventures.*

—Lewis Carroll, *Alice's Adventures in Wonderland*

It was 2001 and I was on the forefront (for once, I was early to something). The internet was the new frontier of dating, the Wild West of love, and I was a pioneer woman. There were prospects galore, with photos and profiles, all of which you could surf, scroll, and search from your computer in the privacy of your own home (this was pre-smartphone days, so all my online dating happened on my laptop in my living room).

My initial reaction was *Holy shit! This is the greatest thing to ever happen to dating!* It was such a cool new concept and technology, I had to try it. I wasn't having any luck in the real world, so I jumped in with both feet and put my trust in JDate to save the day.

## LOOKING FOR LOVE IN
## ALL THE RIGHT PLACES

Much like a real relationship that starts off hot and heavy, so did my relationship with online dating. As I ventured in deeper it quickly turned into a mixed bag: hot, cold, up, down, disappointing, and infuriating all at the same time—not unlike my first online date.

He was cute, around my age; his photos seemed current, he was geographically desirable, and had a gorgeous head of hair. He was also in sports PR, which was an instant bond. I figured if there was no chemistry, at least we could talk about sports. We made a date for drinks at the W Hotel bar in West LA. This was my first foray into online dating, and I was excited.

I arrived at the bar first and found a table in the lounge area. I sat down and waited for him before I ordered my drink. Five minutes went by, then 10, then 15, and still no sign of my JDate.

He was 40 minutes late, but kept texting me on my Blackberry to tell me he was on his way. I ordered a glass of wine and continued to wait. The last text I got was him telling me he didn't want to pay for valet and was circling the block for a parking space. Thoroughly annoyed, I called him and said: "You're already late, why don't you just valet park!?" He reluctantly agreed. I thought to myself, *Really dude, you're 40-something years old, do I really have to tell you how to do this?*

Another 10 minutes passed, and as I was polishing off my wine, he finally walked in. Traipsed in, actually. Sauntered, is more like it. He wasn't in a hurry, that much I could tell. As he casually made his way toward me, I saw that his gorgeous head of hair was actually a bad toupee.

He sat down without offering an apology and launched into some stupid chatter, not taking a breath to ask me a single question, nor showing any contrition for being almost an hour late. (I was the more stupid one for waiting.)

When the waitress came over to take his drink order, he declined. Not even water. I declined a second glass of wine, since I wanted nothing more than to get out of there. The waitress dropped the check on the table and walked off. I looked at it, he looked at it; no one made a move. It was a standoff.

After a few awkward seconds, I pointed to the check. "Are you going to get this or am I?" He didn't budge.

"Well, I guess I've got it then." I pulled out my wallet, put down enough cash to cover the wine and tip, got up, and left him sitting there. Never spoke to him again. Silly me for assuming he'd pay, if only for being a jerk.

## THE LURE OF THAT NEXT CLICK

Online dating is filled with perils, pervs, and some very fine people, too. We've all heard the stories. Sometimes it delivers the goods, sometimes duds. After each dud I'd swear off online dating, only to end up coming back because Mr. Right could be just one click away and God forbid I missed him. It was like a slot machine you couldn't walk away from, lest that last dollar pay off.

When you add in the current day advancements like the game-like rush of swiping, the ego boost of notifications, and the instant gratification of it all, you can see why online dating and dating apps are so addictive.

I never thought online dating and gambling had so much in common until I read that both depend on dopamine to keep people hooked. Dopamine is a chemical neurotransmitter in the body associated with feelings of pleasure and reward. Every time a dater gets a "like" or a slots player gets a jackpot, they get a hit of dopamine. More dopamine, more interaction, and the hits just keep coming.[10]

Even I, a smart, sensible, not-desperate woman and sports bettor, was hooked.

Dating should be fun, but what I discovered with online dating is that it more often feels like a job. All the swiping, scrolling, managing apps, messaging, texting, and vetting potential candidates—then you actually have to meet. You make small talk, size them up, and decide if they're qualified for a full-time gig. It's like being the HR director of your love life.

And you do it because you're single, and it's how the business of love is done. The good news is there's no shame like there was for me in the early days of

---

10    I got this information on Casino.org, "the world's leading online gaming authority," because who better than sick gamblers to talk about the rush, buzz, and high of dating?

internet dating. Back then, when someone asked how you met you'd whisper "online," like it was taboo.

## MAN AND WOMAN CANNOT LIVE ON DATING APPS ALONE!

Dating apps have become so commonplace and ubiquitous that to date any other way is now awkward and weird. People who've grown up in the digital age, in particular, have become so inured to being behind a screen that it's possible they may lose their ability to function in-person altogether. Sadly, romance is all on a keypad. No one even talks on the phone anymore.

I fear everyone's dating and mating muscles are going to atrophy, and if they ever get in front of a real, live human, they won't know what to do with themselves. This is my larger issue with online dating: It's short-circuiting the way humans relate and connect. If we don't use it, we'll lose it.

Here's a creepy scenario: Soon dating will be a video game where you have an avatar that looks like you, and to "meet" someone you go to a VR meeting place. Dating won't even have to be in person; it'll all be in the metaverse, which is great for people with fragile egos and obscene amounts of entitlement who won't do the necessary work of dating. Oh wait. It's already here. Apparently, most of the dating services now have a VR option to meet people. Bizarro world, but oh well (shaking my head and rolling my eyes), whatever it takes to meet the avatar of your dreams!

When I was single it was online dating that was weird and awkward, and meeting someone organically was the norm, if not an everyday occurrence. All you had to do was leave your house. What a concept!

I have a love–hate relationship with dating apps: love them for what they offer, hate them for how they can make you feel. There's so much built-in frustration and baked-in rudeness, you wonder if they're doing more harm than good.

This is my biggest problem with online dating. The frustration and rudeness make you bitter, then you unconsciously carry that bitterness with you as you date, which results in more frustration and bitterness. It's a vicious cycle. When people are mistreated and dates are disposable, we lose our humanity toward each other. That's where online dating loses me.

I know people who've met online and married; I have friends who, if not for dating apps, might not be in relationships right now. But digital dating should be a supplement, not your sole source of love and connection.

## Online Date Like a Pro

When it comes to online dating, if you go into it with an open mind, some thick skin, and the understanding that it might crush your soul, suck the life out of you, and kill your self-esteem, you'll do just fine. If you don't want to risk it, there's always another option: get off the apps, take the AirPods out of your ears, and risk dating the old-fashioned way: by engaging face-to-face, being open to fix-ups, blind dates, and the person in line at Starbucks. There's a meet-cute in your future, but you'll never know unless you put your damn phone down and look up!

## WINNERS AND LOSERS IN THE DATING GAME

The majority of guys I met online were lovely, so I can't complain (maybe because people weren't hardened yet). Some dates became friends, some dates I fixed up with my friends, and some dates I think back on and chuckle.

Like the painfully nervous accountant who downed two martinis in the first 30 minutes of our meeting. Or the struggling writer who, after our one and only dinner date, spent two hours in my bathroom with explosive diarrhea.

Or the dentist-turned-actor who lasted three months—a lifetime in the world of online dating. He didn't just date me; he love-bombed me. He came on strong, romanced me hard, and courted me like there was no tomorrow. Gazing deeply into my eyes on our first date and making me feel like no one else existed should've been my first clue the guy was a love-bombing narcissist.

He was one of a few dates I had after my car accident, and when I recounted my ordeal to him, he took my hand and said with a penetrating look: *"I want to take care of you."*

Everything this guy did told me he was a serious contender. He was boyfriend material from minute one. He acted like a boyfriend, referred to himself as my boyfriend, and didn't flinch when I introduced him as my boyfriend. After spending Thanksgiving with his family, Christmas with mine, and every night together in between, he did something very unboyfriend-like: He dumped me on New Year's Eve.

We were going to my friend's party, getting ready at my house when the bomb was dropped. As I was putting the finishing touches on my makeup, I saw in the vanity mirror reflection that he was lying on my bed, fully clothed in his suit and tie, eyes closed.

I turned around and looked at him. It was an odd sight, him laying on top of my bed in a suit with his shoes on. "Why are you lying down?"

"I'm tired."

We had played tennis a few hours earlier, and he had taken a nap at my place, so I was confused.

"But you already took a nap, why are you still tired?" I was worried he wasn't feeling well. A long pause ensued.

"I don't want to go to the party."

"What do you mean you don't want to go to the party? It's the plan, it's New Year's Eve."

He was quiet for a beat or two, then blurted out: "I'm not sure I want to go out with you anymore."

I was thrown—I mean totally blindsided, not to mention completely speechless. He tried to explain himself.

"You're the serious marrying type, and I feel bad dating you. I want to have fun, and I can't with you."

While the next few minutes of conversation were a blur, I gathered he was giving me a backhanded compliment. He was trying to say that he didn't want to be tied down in a relationship, and I was relationship material, which wasn't fun for him.

Before I told him to go fuck himself, I gave him one last chance to come to his senses.

"We are minutes away from going to my friend's party. It's New Year's Eve, we're both dressed up, we've spent the entire day together, and you're picking right now to break up with me? You couldn't have told me tomorrow, or maybe in a few days?"

He didn't come to his senses, nor did he have a change of heart, so I kicked him out and went to the party by myself. Once there, I drowned my sorrows and stewed. How could I have not seen this coming? He was so earnest, so genuine, so believable—but then again he was an actor, so what did I expect?

At my friend's party, when the clock struck midnight I downed a *glass* of tequila (the equivalent of five shots, probably) and silently bid the a-hole a final farewell. I rang in the new year single again, which wasn't such a hardship since I was usually single on New Year's anyway. It's just another night, I always told myself.

His timing might've been terrible, but at least he wasn't lying. I saw him back online the very next day trolling for more "nonmarrying" types to have fun with.

## TROLLING FOR THE TRUTH

I was trolling, too—for a serious boyfriend, with serious intentions—which was a tough task, since so many people lie online about who they are and what they want. In my experience the online dater is 10 years older, 20 pounds heavier, and a few inches shorter than what their profile says.

I realized this when I met an online date for happy hour at a crowded after-work bar. Going by my date's profile picture (dark hair, no glasses), I scanned the place but couldn't find him. A minute later, a much older man with thinning gray hair, who had been practically right in front of my face the entire time, introduced himself. It was my date, but he looked nothing like his profile picture. He looked like my grandpa with little round spectacles.

Not that older men aren't attractive; they are. So are short men, bald men, men with bellies, men with imperfections and character. The problem is that some men (and a lot of women too) feel the need to misrepresent themselves online. A woman with some curves, a little gray, maybe a few wrinkles is sexy, so why hide it?

We all want to be someone's type; we all want to be swiped on. We all want to be wanted and should do everything we can to put our best face forward. But starting off with a fib sets a bad precedent. Eventually the truth will come out, and your real age, height, weight, smile lines, and paunch will be seen.

You know what's really attractive? Honesty. You know what's really hot? Showing the real you. Showing the real you isn't just refreshing—it speaks volumes about having the courage to be yourself.

For as many people who lie about their personal attributes, there are just as many who lie about their true relationship status. These are mostly men you suspect are still married or are juggling multiple women. You know this because they text more than they talk. They text all the time, at all hours, and will not pick up the phone to save their life. Sometimes they'll pop up on social media to compliment you, or slide into your DMs just to keep you guessing. This manipulative practice is known as "breadcrumbing" because of the demoralizing trail of crumbs they leave (and the more demoralizing assumption that you'll accept such crumbs). Guys like this also use their kids, jobs, or travel schedule to get out of having to actually speak.

Note to the ladies: If you meet a guy online (or anywhere else for that matter) who prefers to *text and not talk*, do yourself a favor and *run don't walk*.

For me, each of these dating experiences, although comical at times, helped narrow my search for love. Like I said, knowing what you don't want is just as important as knowing what you do want. Being online just shows it to you faster.

## HACK YOUR WAY TO DATING SUCCESS

If you're ready to head into the Wild West of online dating (or have been out West for a while and want better results) here are my dating hacks:

1. Don't live on your dating apps, and don't date like your life depends on it. Dating apps are a 1.17-billion-dollar business for a reason. They're designed to keep you searching, spending time and money. Whether you're buying premium subscriptions, making monthly payments, or seeing ads, apps are making money from you. Realize that the more sinister

M.O. of apps is to keep you single, so don't let it hold you hostage. Allow yourself a specific amount of time to engage, then go about your life.

2. Don't let the sheer number of online daters overwhelm or paralyze you. This is known as the "paradox of choice." Having endless options makes it harder to choose.

3. Keep your standards high and your expectations low so you're never disappointed.

4. As mentioned, be truthful with your age, weight, height, and what you're looking for. Use current pictures. Don't start off with a lie.

5. Present your best self. Make an effort. Guys, clean up; ladies, put on some lipstick. Get some high-quality photos taken, and post three (including headshot and full length). No bathroom selfies, and no overfiltering, please! You only have a couple seconds to make an impression, so make it a good one (but a natural one too).

6. You don't need to be a Pulitzer Prize–winning author to write a dating profile or craft a semi-interesting message to someone. All it requires is a little thought, some personalization, and your own unique voice.

7. Be honest when stating your goals and intentions, but don't make too many demands or have too many conditions. If you want a LTR (long-term relationship) or FWB (friends with benefits), make it clear. Don't bait and switch.

8. Get that chip off your shoulder, otherwise you'll come off looking bitchy, bossy, or bitter—which will send suitors running for the hills. Being pre-emptively aggro screams that you've been hurt and expect to be hurt again.

9. Addendum to #7: Saying "no drama" in your profile signals you've had too much of it, and most likely are a cause of it.

10. Exchange a few texts or calls, then meet your date as soon as possible. Communicating for days or weeks on end with someone can never live up to the hype when you finally meet.

11. Don't pin all your hopes on or invest too heavily in one person too soon. That goes for dating IRL, too.

12. Conversely, don't toss someone back too fast just because there are plenty of fish on the apps. Hang in there for a minute, see where it goes.

13. If you're getting burned out, deactivate your accounts and do a digital detox. Don't be afraid of missing out. If your person is out there, they will make themselves known.

14. Don't be so fast to post a budding relationship on social media. If things don't work out, there's nothing more embarrassing than having to unfriend, block, and announce you're splitsville soon after posting you're a couple.

15. Don't trash your ex, online or off, and make a mental note if your date trashes their ex—it's always a tip-off to bigger anger and resentment issues.

16. Never view a bad date as a waste of time; instead, see them as opportunities to learn something or make adjustments. Bad dates can make great stories, so relish the comic gold they give you. As I always say: "Do it for the story!"

17. Online dating may be visual, but try not to be shallow. Train yourself to get past looks. Date against type and give someone a chance. That skinny, zaftig, geeky, older, younger, goofy, bald, dreadlocked person on Bumble could end up being the next love of your life.

18. We're all in this together, so date with kindness and empathy.

19. Think of online dating not just as a way to find love, but also to network, broaden your horizons and make new friends or business contacts. Even if it's not a match, it could lead to something else.

20. Assume you will get ghosted, benched, paperclipped, or any other abhorrent dating word of the moment (there will be hundreds more by the time this book comes out). Because of the anonymous nature of online dating, bad behavior is a given. Yes, you'll get angry, but you'll survive. Remember, no one ever died from being breadcrumbed.

21. If you know there's no second date and you're not a match, say so. Be proactive, gracious, and save them face. Thank them for their time and wish them all the best.

22. Don't take online dating too seriously or personally. If you don't roll with the punches and keep your sense of humor, you'll go from dater to hater faster than a left swipe on Tinder.

For as much as we now know about digital dating, it's still the Wild West of love, where anything can happen—good, bad, and ugly. There are people to meet, experiences to be had, stories to be told, and quite possibly, love to be found. It might feel like work sometimes, but if you're less HR director and more Alice in Wonderland, you can make it an adventure and not a job.

# TEST-DRIVEN TAKEAWAY

The dopamine rush of online dating isn't just addictive; it can create a digital dependency that breeds poor social skills and bad manners. And it's not just happening with younger demographics. People over 50 are picking up bad habits and forgetting their manners, too. To my post-50 cohort: Dating may be at the touch of a fingertip these days, but there's a big difference between convenience and a crutch. So don't be lazy or rude, and don't stay behind your screens. You must make real connections IRL—not just for yourself, but for mankind too. People like to feel seen, heard, and acknowledged, and you'll be doing humanity a great service by creating good vibes in the world. It will also make YOU feel good. Remember, you're from a generation that actually knows how to look someone in the eye and speak, so I'm counting on you.

# DATING BEST PRACTICES, LATE-BLOOMER STYLE

*Just that you do the right thing. The rest does not matter.*

—Epictetus

I had my first date at 14 and didn't stop dating till I was 50. I've been on all kinds of dates: coffee dates, drink dates, hiking dates, lunch dates, dinner dates, tennis dates; even a ride to my car mechanic counted as a date.

I once had a date with a guy who got stung by a scorpion and spent the rest of the evening with him in the ER. I even met a guy at jury duty whom I dated for a bit. Along with driving ranges, yoga studios, dog parks, coffee houses, sports bars, school reunions, pickleball, and home improvement stores, jury duty is the world's greatest place to meet people. It's a captive audience (with singles for sure) and you're stuck there all day, so I'd think twice before getting out of it.

When it comes to dating, you could say I've been around the block a few times. Enough times to realize that some dating traditions, as old as they may be, never go out of style. In fact, they stand the test of time. Men will be men, women will be women, and human nature doesn't really change all that much when it comes to romance and courtship.

I said the word "courtship"; that should tell you how old-fashioned I am.

At the risk of sounding like an old lady, that's just who I am when it comes to dating. My best practices are from another era. I think ladies should be ladylike and men should be gentlemen. I think Led Zeppelin is the greatest rock band of all time, and no one will ever be funkier than Earth, Wind & Fire in the 1970s. I prefer phone calls to texts, dating IRL to dating apps, and my biggest cause célèbre, I prefer shopping in stores to shopping online—if only for reasons having to do with dating. Online shopping isn't just replacing brick and mortar retail (which is sad), even sadder, it's slowly eliminating our traditional meeting spots, gathering places, and social spaces, which in turn, reduces opportunities for organic connection. It is turning our downtowns into ghost towns. Less foot traffic means less human interaction. If any city planners are reading this, I beg you to keep single people in mind when designing walkable communities and urban centers. Thank you!

Back to my rant: I think posting half-naked selfies is tacky, sending dick pics is classless, and hookup culture is the Decline of Western Civilization Part I. However, because we're experiencing an epidemic of loneliness and isolation these days, it's actual sex that is in decline. Apparently, we're not having enough of it.

According to recent studies, adults of all ages, demographics, relationship and economic statuses, are having less sex than they have had at any point in at least the past three decades. Back in the '60s and '70s, we called hookup culture "free love," and it was pretty groovy. No one complained! I say it's time to make sex groovy again!

OK, Boomer! (But on the tail end of boomer, so technically I'm not that old and stodgy.)

No shock here that some of my dating best practices will seem ridiculously outdated, controversial, even sexist. You'll either roll your eyes, gag, laugh in my face, or call the anti-feminism police on me, and I'm prepared.

Even if I lose followers or get flamed on Twitter, I stand by my embarrassingly archaic beliefs.

## MATRIMANIA

On the other hand, some of my best practices will sound like the proud and progressive dater I was for most of my life. When you're perpetually single like I was, you have to be your own champion. However, as much as I advocated for myself as an assertive single female, I also advocated for proper dating conventions and virtues, and still do to this day. Some things endure.

Being proudly and unapologetically single—by choice or chance—makes a statement, especially in a world obsessed with coupledom. Maybe one day marriage will become obsolete, but for now it's still considered the ultimate prize. There's even a word for it: *matrimania*, the glorifying of marriage and coupling. (Confession: I suffered with chronic matrimania for years, which I was convinced was incurable.)

The world is changing, though, and so are relationships, gender roles, and identity. At the same time, the dos and don'ts of dating are also changing. Back when I was single, we read the book *The Rules* and followed it like it was gospel.[11] Now the rules seem archaic.

Or do they? Can old-school dating traditions hold up in a no-rules dating world? Is the notion that modern women should wait for men to take the lead antiquated or on point? Are masculine and feminine archetypes a thing of the past, or things to be considered when dating?

Like I said, I've seen it all and dated it all, but my advice isn't gospel, one-size-fits-all, or written in stone. There are no hard and fast rules. Dating style and sexual preferences are individual and unique, and results may vary.

So for the sake of this conversation, I'm speaking as a middle-aged heterosexual woman with one foot in the 1950s and one in the twenty-first century.

---

11   Ellen Fein and Sherrie Schneider, *The Rules: Time-Tested Secrets for Capturing the Heart of Mr. Right* (New York: Grand Central Publishing, 1995).

Here are my O.G. dating philosophies, with updates for our current times.

## MAKING THE FIRST MOVE

I already told you how my mother felt about not pursuing men, and for better or for worse, it got into my head. In her dating times men made the first move, and in my dating times, I still believe it's the right move—to a point.

Thanks to modern feminism and dating apps, women are making the first move more than ever. Men definitely appreciate it when a woman initiates. But here's where things get scientific: Men are primal and are wired to hunt. They like the chase and don't like easy prey.

According to psychologist Dr. Duana C. Welch, PhD, author of the Love Factually series, the original science-based dating advice books, we can blame evolution for this. When I interviewed her for this chapter she told me that modern dating behaviors date back to caveman days, when mating rituals and psychology were first wired in. Not surprisingly, women have a lot to do with this.

> We women are the ones who say "yes" or "no" to sexual access— and we always were, back to the first men and women. All scientific signs are that ancestral women were likelier to get it on with men who vanquished other men in competitions, and the most important competition for heterosexual men is getting sexual with women.
>
> Our ancestral mothers—the ones we are directly descended from—literally shaped men's mating psychology by choosing some men over others. Ancestral women, like women today, preferred men who threw themselves into competition, and won.
>
> Men who were often picked became ancestors; men who never got selected became memories. So men today want to compete—at work, on the ballfield, and for your heart. What does this mean for you? Don't take their job away! Let them

pursue you. Let them pay for dinner. Let them know you're dating around. Let them wait for full sexual access to you. It's a two-fer: It gives you valuable information about whether this guy is looking at you long-term (since being hard-to-get drives away players) and it gives men the thrill of the chase. Oh, and it gives both of you what we all want: a shot at lasting love.[12]

This theory was offered up again in a book I read when I was down-on-my-luck single and grasping for anything to help me. *Getting to "I Do,"* by relationship expert and author Patricia Allen, was an eye-opener.[13] It gave me insight into the male species and changed the way I dated.

According to Allen, every man has a feminine feeling side, and every woman has a masculine thinking side. You can either be a feminine-energy, receptive, cherished woman, or an assertive, respected, masculine-energy woman. The key is knowing which one you are.

Allen asserts that whoever makes the first move unknowingly chooses to be the male in the relationship. When a woman approaches a man, she unconsciously and automatically sets up the relationship.

My guess is that strong, independent women of my ilk, even though we're female, often take the male pursuer role because, well, we're strong and independent.

Looking back at my relationships, I was a feminine-energy woman trapped inside a masculine-energy body. I started off as a feminine-energy female, but soon after, my male energy would kick in and completely change the dating dynamic.

For example, if I met a guy at a party, I'd be female and let them approach me. I'd give them my number, and they'd proceed to pursue me, with little effort on my end. But as we got closer I'd change tack, making the relationship more

---

12   Interview with Welch, March 2022.

13   Patricia Allen, *Getting to "I Do": The Secret to Doing Relationships Right!* (New York: William Morrow, 1995).

about them, not about me. I presented a version of myself I thought they wanted me to be, and as a result, I lost the confidence to be my authentic self.

I thought by being low-maintenance and nondemanding, I'd be that much more attractive and win their affections. Not only did that not happen, it backfired. I wasn't demanding enough! For someone who's never at a loss for words, I lost the ability to communicate my needs. The men I dated got all the nurturing and cherishing, but when I needed it, it was nowhere to be found. I may have been respected, but I wasn't being cherished.

In *Getting to "I Do,"* Allen asks: "Do you want to be cherished for your feelings or respected for your thoughts? If you want to be respected first, you will choose to be the 'male energy.' If you want to be cherished first, you will choose to be the 'female' energy." True female energy, as I now know it, is the ability to be strong *and* vulnerable. . . .

Allen follows up with this advice: "If you choose to be female, flirt with your eyes and smile, and let him pursue you."

I've always used eye contact and a smile as my trusty ice breakers. They signal you're open and approachable, but so is saying hello in line at the grocery store or making small talk in an elevator. As I mentioned earlier, everywhere you go is an opportunity to make a connection. To get in the habit of smiling, when you're out and about, keep the corners of your mouth slightly turned up. It's not only a welcome sign to others; it guards against resting bitch face.

## Flirt Like a Pro

Along with flirting with your eyes and smiling, there are other subtle ways to show interest and get the ball rolling. If you're game to make the first move, here are some pointers:

- Small talk goes a long way. Asking questions, chatting, or commiserating with someone establishes connection and chemistry.
- Drop hints and clues you're single and not seeing anyone.
- A friendly touch on the arm establishes intimacy and warmth.

- Once you've established rapport with someone, invite them to coffee, or include them in a casual group setting with your friends.
- Or just ask them out on a real date and screw my advice.

Making the first move is bold; the key is to limit any weirdness or possible rejection that might come with it. So keep it light, with no pressure, and if your vibe isn't returned, pat yourself on the back for trying and keep smiling.

Actually, my problem isn't with who flirts first; it's with those who don't flirt at all or the people who let their phones do the flirting for them. This goes back to the alienation digital dating creates: Yes, it brings people together, but it also keeps them apart. Dating apps give socially awkward and lazy people an easy out. Introverts, I feel your pain, but you're not off the hook here.

**To get in the habit of smiling, when you're out and about, keep the corners of your mouth slightly turned up.**

Flirting is fundamental to dating. When we don't flirt, we forget how; when we forget how, we think we don't need to flirt in the first place. And that's my fear, that flirting is becoming extinct.

Nothing can replace flirting. No dating app can mimic real, in-person, chemistry-establishing, face-to-face interaction. Before you say, "But I flirt by text!" sorry, that doesn't count. Smiley faces and heart emojis are no substitute for getting an immediate vibe with someone.

Because we're in a flirting crisis, I'm calling for an all-out effort to bring it back, by any means necessary. The situation is dire, so I'll start by putting aside my old-fashioned views and encourage everyone to start flirting ASAP. Tradition be damned! Bat your eyes, chat someone up, hold their gaze, drop your hankie, just do something. I don't care if you're a man or woman, both sexes can send signals and initiate. There's no more standing on ceremony, no more excuses.

Both sexes have the power, and gender roles are much more flexible. Plus, flirting (along with most dating/mating behaviors) is primal, as we know, so we can't let technology do for us what we should be doing ourselves—and have been doing for the last many million years.

Flirting is the heavy lifting of dating. Yes, it takes guts, but as I said in the last chapter, either use it or lose it.

## HAVING SEX TOO SOON

We don't wait for anything these days. Our on-demand culture expects everything *now*, at the click of a button, including dating. But just because we live in an instant gratification world doesn't mean you have to instantly give it up.

You already know how I feel about sex: It's good for the social fabric, good for human connection, and it's groovy. Here's my caveat though: If you're starting to date someone new and feel there's potential, slow your roll. A slow build is seductive, keeping some mystery is hot, and taking your time is the best foreplay of all. Waiting to jump into the sack allows you to get to know each other and establishes trust, which will give your courtship and budding relationship more staying power. Plus, in the age of #MeToo, taking your time will prevent any potential misunderstandings or issues with consent.

The problem with having sex too soon is that the relationship becomes all about the sex, and not enough about the person. I know people who've had sex on the first date and got married, but I wouldn't chance it. Again, that's just me being older and wiser. Having sex too soon can not only undermine a potential relationship; but it can also sabotage your self-esteem. Because after a conquest, there's little incentive for a guy to keep pursuing you. Remember, I'm on Team Caveman here.

Remember also, that sex can cloud your judgment. It can make you think you're in love and that the person you're banging is your soulmate, but really, it's your body's love drug oxytocin talking. When the buzz wears off, you're looking at a totally different person.

Now, if a one-nighter, friend with benefits, or no-strings hookup is what you want and need, by all means do it. Casual sex does serve a purpose. Like if you've been in a sexless marriage and crave physical touch, or newly single and need to get laid, or widowed and need a warm body, or horny and need some action, I won't stop you. But if you're going through a breakup, feeling vulnerable, maybe fragile, and need some love, I *will* stop you. Because the best way to get over someone isn't to get under them; the best way to get over someone is to keep your clothes on until you're fully healed.

Here's another reason to wait till you're fully healed: the possibility it may all backfire. Nothing will make you run back to your ex faster than bad sex with someone else. Especially after you've made progress, you don't want a massive setback.

And to those who think it's a good idea to have sex with someone on the first date to establish chemistry or compatibility. Do you see my head exploding? If there's anything that will make Church Lady here lose her shit, it's the notion that it's best to get sex out of the way first to see if you want to keep dating that person. Arrgh!

Bottom line, if you want someone to know you for *you* first, if you want them to want you *after* getting intimate, I'd say wait.

## PLAYING HARD TO GET

Remember the three-day rule of when to call? Now it's turned into "How long should I wait to return a text?" Things don't change.

If you want the answer, ask a high-value woman. A high-value woman is someone who understands her importance and worth and shows it with quiet confidence and restraint. She doesn't wait by the phone ready to pounce on the next call, text, or notification she gets within seconds of receiving it.

One of my mom's trademark pieces of advice was to never answer the phone on the first ring, so as not to appear too eager. This was before cell phones, but still, she had the right idea.

I consider my mother high-value because she knew her worth as a single woman. She didn't make herself too available, nor did she make dating her highest priority. She had other things to do, like raising me and building her business.

High-value women value themselves, their time, their heart, and the life they have outside of dating. When a woman makes herself too available, it signals to potential suitors that she's easy and her love doesn't need to be earned.

Is this playing hard to get? No. It's *being* hard to get. Big difference.

Duana Welch clarifies:

> "Hard to get" is not being aloof or cold or bitchy. It's not being an ice queen. It's about controlling the pacing of the sexual relationship, and refusing to be treated like an option rather than a priority. So if he calls you at the last minute to get together, you say, I'm so sorry. I've got plans. Don't allow yourself to be treated like someone who can be had at the last minute. That's not hard to get. That's putting yourself firmly in option territory. And men respond with respect to priority territory.[14]

In case you think this is passive-aggressive, consider the study in the *Journal of Social and Personal Relationships* that shows "mate value" increases when you're hard to get. When the chase is harder, it increases a potential mate's desirability. The authors discovered that immediately reciprocating another person's interest may not be the smartest strategy for attracting mates.[15]

According to the study, people who are too easy to attract may be perceived as more desperate, which makes them less valuable and appealing than those who don't make their romantic interest apparent right away.

We always want what we can't have, right? And the harder we have to work

---

14    Interview with Welch, March 2022.

15    Gurit E. Birnbaum, Kobi Zholtack, and Harry T. Reis, "No Pain, No Gain: Perceived Partner Mate Value Mediates the Desire-Inducing Effect of Being Hard to Get During Online and Face-to-Face Encounters," *Journal of Social and Personal Relationships*, June 4, 2020, https://journals.sagepub.com/eprint/J6I6GX95ZFWIPGIATRF7/full.

for it, the more precious it appears, the more we want it. Well, the same principle applies to dating.

Three days is too long, if you ask me. It reeks of manipulation and insecurity. Whether it's a text, email, call, or dating app message, answer within a decent amount of time. A healthy relationship is built on mutual effort, so be responsive, show interest, and don't make people guess. That's a really low-value move.

## TALKING POLITICS ON THE FIRST DATE

Back in the day, you didn't discuss politics or religion, but that was before Donald Trump. Today, your politics are your values, and your values are your politics. I don't care if it's unsavory; talking politics on a first date must be done. Whether it's climate change, women's rights, or baby-eating pedophiles, it's important to know where someone stands on the issues.

To illustrate what a hot button issue this is, dating website OKCupid did a survey and found that 60% of respondents would not date someone whose political views were opposite of theirs. This means that "Libtards" will not be dating "Repugnants" any time soon. Unless you're on the same page politically, amazingly open-minded, or are too horny to care, politics is a complete boner killer.

Most people state their politics upfront on their profiles, which makes things clear. (Does "Swipe left if you voted for Trump" ring a bell?) However, if you're on a date and still don't know on which side of the aisle they sit, find out. Ask questions, probe a bit. You'll either establish a fast sympatico, or you'll devolve into a mud-slinging shouting match. Should you opt for the latter, don't bother trying to change anyone's mind. They're dug in, you're dug in—better you both knock back your cocktails and call it a night.

However, if you find yourself with someone on the opposite side who's respectful of your views and can intelligently convey their views too, you may have an interesting start to something. This, though, will be the rare exception and not the rule.

## SPLITTING THE CHECK
## AND OTHER GESTURES

As a proud feminist, I believe in equal rights, equal pay, and an equal playing field for women. I'll fight for it and march for it, but when it comes to feminism in dating I draw the line—or at least, I bend the rules. Modern feminism isn't just completely at odds with traditional romance; it's completely at odds with how I feel.

Let's talk about a guy paying vs. splitting the check. Somehow, it's become a third rail in dating. In my playbook, paying for a woman on a first date is a class move, not to mention, the courtly thing to do. It's also proper etiquette. If someone asks you out on a date, and it's their idea, technically they should pay.

To those who scoff at men paying, or think dating is misogynistic in general, you shouldn't be dating. There's nothing wrong with demanding equality, but dating isn't a battle of the sexes. It's not a competition. You can have a job, make your own money, and take care of yourself while appreciating timeless acts of chivalry at the same time. Letting a man pay is a time-honored tradition. So is holding the door open, pulling out your chair, and opening the car door for you. It's not toxic masculinity—it's good manners.

Accepting kind gestures won't kill your independent spirit, weaken you as a woman, or render you a Stepford wife. In fact, the opposite will happen. You'll be seen as someone secure enough to allow herself to be treated well.

**It's not toxic masculinity—it's good manners.**

I realize there are bad guys out there . . . weirdos, scammers, narcissists, predators, abusers . . . and women should be on the lookout. You should always be vigilant, always protect yourself. Sexism and harassment are rampant; so is entitlement, selfishness, and a general lack of empathy in dating. Even the smartest and savvy of us can fall victim.

Bad behavior cannot be normalized. Men, you can do better. Women, you deserve better.

With that said, we need to remember that not all men are bad. Not everyone you date is out to get you, and the patriarchy isn't always out to take you down. There are good men out there who want to do the right thing when it comes to romance, so try to put social progress aside for a minute and let them woo you.

## FEMINISTS, STOP GETTING YOUR KNICKERS IN A KNOT!

Courting is an ancient ritual, a beautiful dance, and as I mentioned, a soon-to-be lost art if we're not careful, so stop getting your feminist knickers in a knot! We all know you don't need a free meal and can open your own door. Furthermore, if a man approaches you in a respectful and tactful way, it's not a crime against humanity. It's called being "hit on," and it's a compliment. Even if you're not interested, at least give the brave soul who does approach you some credit instead of giving them grief. It's not easy putting yourself out there and risking rejection, if not worse.

Dating in a post-MeToo world has pretty much killed cold approaching for men. Women want to be left alone, and men got the hint. For better or for worse, the dating power dynamics have shifted; maybe not for boomers (because who doesn't like getting hit on at this age?!) but definitely for younger generations. Between women not needing men and men going their own way, it's a total shit show out there.

I once read an article on the demise of masculine empowerment, and in the comments section was this gem: "Radical feminism has served to pathologize all forms of masculinity as public health hazard." Good job, girls!

To be fair, toxic masculinity has earned its equal place in many a comment section, as evidenced by this pearl of wisdom from a man: "I have one thing to say to men. There is no greater destroyer of desire or libido than resentment. Keep that in mind, and pretty soon, you will all find yourselves in weekend circle jerks. Forever." Way to go, guys!

When guys send unsolicited dick pics we know male entitlement is out of control, and when women bash guys for hitting on them, we know feminism has gone off the rails. When both sexes undermine their causes by being jerks or gold-diggers, we know dating is doomed. No wonder everyone is resentful and pointing fingers.

Because romance is on the verge of extinction, we need to preserve it, not rail against it. There's an old saying women would exclaim when a man did something romantic: "Chivalry is not dead!" For this generation, and generations to come, chivalry must be kept alive and well. We also need to keep decency, kindness, and *love* alive too.

Just so you know, in terms of reciprocation, my traditional gender role only goes so far. I've paid for meals, initiated plans, and pulled out my wallet on many occasions, and it was my pleasure to do so. I was a modern woman who worked, made her own money, and didn't stand on ceremony. In the early stages of dating, though, I'd let the guy pay, and the pleasure was all his. The least I could do was to offer to pay for ice cream or a drink after, which was very appreciated.

As for money and love, as you continue to date and a relationship develops, depending on your finances (and his) you can show your feminism in future dates by reciprocating. You'll figure it out as you go along.

The only caveat I'd offer about the guy paying on a first date is that if you know there's not going to be a second date, then pay for yourself. Split the check so there's no hard feelings or expectations beyond dinner. And by expectations, I mean sex. Guys, I don't care if it's a cup of coffee or a five-course dinner you're paying for, no one owes you sex. Full stop.

Dating shouldn't be mutual destruction. Men and women need to stop oppressing each other and start celebrating each other. We need to appreciate that not every man is an alpha male, and not every woman wants to break your balls. Feminine-energy women aren't sellouts to their gender, and humble men aren't weak. In fact, they're adorable. If a humble introvert came up to me when I was single and said, "I'm really shy, but I'd like to get to know you," I'd rip my clothes off right there and then.

Sometimes confidence is overrated—it's humility that's the ultimate panty-dropper.

—

I took a big chance sharing some of my dating best practices with you, seeing as most of them are relics from the Stone Age. Hopefully, though, after you roll your eyes, gag, or laugh in my face, you'll put them into practice and see that I'm right. And if you still want to call the anti-feminism police on me, go right ahead. Remember, I'm a proud feminist, a progressive former dater, a high-value woman, and a masculine-energy female. Chicks like us can handle anything.

# EIGHT

# LATE TO THE GAME,
# BUT STILL A PLAYER

*It's not about the cards you're dealt, but how you play the hand.*
—Randy Pausch, *The Last Lecture*

Before I was married, I kept a very full and diverse dating portfolio. I met interesting people, went to interesting places, flew on private planes, was treated like a princess—and my anti-princess side didn't protest. At heart, I'm a girl's girl who loves all things girly, like getting mani-pedis, lunching with the ladies, and playing mah-jongg. But I'm also a guy's girl who can spend all day in a Vegas sportsbook laying the points, taking the dog, and betting the moneyline. I'm just as at home hanging with my homegirls as I am hanging with the guys.

By most single girl standards, you could say I was highly unconventional. I was a player, as they say. In fact, I was more of a player than most players—just ask my bookie.

My dating portfolio also included sex. Good sex, bad sex, and funny sex. In a crazier single girl moment, I had sex with a boyfriend inside his Jeep while parked at an old Westward Ho grocery store (now Whole Foods), which of course gives new meaning to the expression "Westward ho."

If you want to get a quick glimpse into my single days, check out this decades-old text conversation between my friend-since-grammar school Dodd, and his friend "Phil" (name changed), with whom I supposedly had a date, but can't remember.

**PHIL:** Whatsup dodd . . . smell my finger. How do you know treva brandon

**DODD:** Know TB since I was 10. How do you know her?

**PHIL:** Went out with her once about 10 yrs ago. Forgot how we met. She had a long distance thing with a guy in CO . . . spent 60 bucks, didnt even get a kiss just attitude

**DODD:** Too bad must have been you

**PHIL:** yeah right

**DODD:** She's no town pump. Obviously your date would confirm that

**PHIL:** town pump . . . lol

**DODD:** She's probably too picky

**PHIL:** so i try to reconnect wth her on fb, tells me again shes seeing someone and doesnt remember me . . . douche

**DODD:** HAHA let it go man. She's TREVA fucking Brandon

**PHIL:** what the f does that mean

**DODD:** She's legendary. I've loved her from afar for 39 years

**PHIL:** good lord

**DODD:** Don't take it personally. The 60 bucks is gone. Let it go . . .

Oh my gosh Phil, as funny as this text is, I'm mortified you felt this way. I'm sorry it wasn't a match, and I'm sorry you spent so much money on me. As a gesture of goodwill though, I'm happy to refund your 60 bucks and fix you up with one of my single girlfriends. I won't smell your finger, though.

If you're wondering what kept me in the game all those years, it was my intrepid spirit. Having a sense of adventure and natural curiosity—not to mention ridiculous athletic-level stamina and endurance—enabled me to see dating as a walkabout and not hard labor on a prison chain gang. I was a hopeful romantic who could go the distance.

Logan Ury, director of relationship science at the dating app Hinge, reminds her dating coaching clients to "A.B.F.: Always Be Flirting"—a great piece of advice, but I'd also add "A.B.C.: Always Be Curious," because curiosity is what's going to give your dating life longevity.[16]

The best part of dating for me was making new connections. If I connected with someone and there was a spark, I'd get their birth info, then run home and do a chart to see if we were a match. If their Mars was conjunct my Venus, or my Sun trined their Moon, or we had a composite 7th house Jupiter, it was on. If I got to Date #3 and it looked promising, I'd consult my astrologer Spencer for a deeper dive (FYI, he has a file of every wannabe, has-been, and almost-boyfriend I've ever had).

My single days were like the Roaring 20s . . . then 30s . . . then 40s. But when I hit 43 the roaring ceased, the party ended, and the runaway girlfriend stopped in her tracks.

That's when my biological clock went off, and the fun and frolic came to a screeching halt. In one fell swoop, I hated being single, needed a husband, and wanted kids ASAP. I literally woke up one morning out of the blue panic-stricken and suddenly and painfully aware of time.

In astrology, they call this panic your "Uranus Return," when the planet Uranus—known as the planet of change, shock, and disruption—traverses 180 degrees from the position it was at the time of your birth. This event occurs at approximately 42 years old, and acts as a midlife checkpoint, or "midlife crisis." Everyone who hits this age feels it in some form. For me it was like a wake-up call or an alarm going off, which in true late-bloomer form, went off late. Most women's bio clocks go off in their 30s. Not mine. The thought of getting married and having babies then, when my fertility was at its peak, was far from my mind, but when I hit 43, my mind couldn't think of anything else except getting married and having babies.

A ticking clock does strange things to a person. It fills you with angst, skews your judgment, and lowers your standards—all of which happened when my biological alarm sounded.

---

16    Logan Ury, "Logan Says You're Dating All Wrong," *New York Times*, June 9, 2022, https://www.nytimes.com/2022/06/09/well/live/logan-ury-dating-advice.html.

## MY RENEWED MANHUNT

Suddenly, dating became an imperative that sent me on a husband manhunt. With my bar at an all-time low, I ended up going out with practically every unavailable idiot in town, because I was in a hurry and had no time to be picky. If they were damaged goods, I dated them; if they were broken, I'd fix them. My criteria was: If you had a pulse and a penis, you were marriage material.

If a guy was emotionally fucked up, he became my project and I'd go full trainer, employing all my motivational strategies to get him into emotional shape. Just as I handled my father's post-divorce grief, I took on their pain and suffering like a coaching job. The difference was that once they got strong, they'd thank me and go marry someone else. These guys are called "foster boyfriends" for a reason, because after I dated them, they'd go find their forever homes.

From age 40 to 50, I lost my direction, my standards, and myself. Dating, which had once been the thrill of victory, became the agony of defeat.

The bulk of the guys I dated during this time were mostly one-hit wonders; others went three and out; none could close the deal. And mostly all of them were divorced.

Beware the bait and switch from the newly divorced guys.

Newly divorced guys tell you everything you want to hear because they're 1) lonely, 2) horny, 3) selfish, 4) on the rebound, and 5) not in their right mind. They're never serious about becoming serious. They throw just enough bait out there to keep you swimming.

**From age 40 to 50, I lost my direction, my standards, and myself.**

And if they have kids, prepare for more challenges. When you're with a divorced dad or single mom, you will never come first. Get used to it and respect it, because that's the way it should be. I say this as a child of divorce. My mother and father might have had a complicated history, but when it came to parenting, they always put me first.

I know all too well that divorced guys are complicated. Like the newly divorced fellow I was starting to date who began weeping the one and only time we fooled around. In the middle of what was supposed to be a passionate moment, he put his head in his hands and began to cry.

ME: Are you OK?

HIM: I just can't do it.

I'm thinking to myself: *Can't do what? Get it up?* I waited for a break in his sobs to glean more information.

HIM: I just don't have the emotional bandwidth to be in a relationship right now.

These were the early days of dial-up internet service, and I had no idea what "bandwidth" meant, but I sensed it wasn't good. He tearfully explained that he hadn't processed his divorce and didn't want more kids, even though he had reassured me repeatedly that he did. That's when I started crying.

Suffice to say, most divorced guys are not in a rush to marry a woman with a loudly ticking biological clock who's never been married and wants kids like, yesterday. I can't really blame them.

Before I go on bashing divorced guys—or ambivalent people in general—I need to point something out.

Maybe they're ambivalent for a reason. Maybe they're perfectly wonderful, and really do dig you, but they're not ready to commit. Maybe they need to play the field, sow their wild oats, or heal their hearts. And how can I not relate, seeing as I wasn't ready for the longest time, and was often ambivalent myself? I can hardly point fingers here.

But still, dating these types gave me PTSD because I always feared the other shoe was going to drop.

Many years before, my good friend Kathie gave me a cute little needlepoint pillow for my birthday that said, "Star light, star bright, where oh where is Mr. Right?" I must've asked myself that a million times.

Silly me used to think Mr. Right was right around the corner, or at least somewhere in the vicinity. I just assumed he'd show up and we'd get married, no sweat. But Mr. Right wasn't right around the corner; he was a million miles away, and that's when I started to sweat.

The harder I searched, the further he stayed away, the more I was sweating. Mr. Right may have been MIA, but there were other misters who did show up in his place, including but not limited to:

- Mr. Successful, but emotionally stunted
- Mr. Middle-Aged with arrested development
- Mr. Harvard Grad and total moron
- Mr. Psychotherapist with commitment phobia

None of these were Mr. Right, and I knew it. I would curse the universe: "Where the @#*! is Mr. Right?" Unfortunately the universe didn't deliver him, but it did deliver the truth: If a guy was a total moron or emotionally stunted, had arrested development or commitment phobia, he wasn't Mr. Right, and never would be.

## DO YOU HAVE THE RIGHT STUFF?

I want women to meet Mr. Right, and I want men to be Mr. Right. I root for men to do the right thing, and I want women to follow suit. Because when it comes down to it, you all want the same thing: honesty, decency, and respect.

To know if someone's right for you, consider the following:

> **Mr. Right wasn't right around the corner; he was a million miles away.**

1. **They know how to communicate.** They aren't afraid to express their feelings, thoughts, goals, or anything else. They're honest about who they are and encourage you to be honest too.

2. **They don't try to get to know you through texting.** Someone who's interested calls. They don't hide behind texts or carry on day-long text conversations that go nowhere. Too much gets lost in translation when you text anyway, so keep it to a minimum when just starting out.

3. **They would move heaven and earth to see you.** Or as an old friend of mine put it, "If a guy wants you, he'll put his dick through glass." In lieu of a dick, if a woman wants you, she'll stop jerking you around with flimsy excuses to get out of seeing you. If she means business, she'll make you a priority.

4. **They pursue you properly.** They make plans, they think ahead, and they don't wait till the last minute to ask you out. They're inquisitive, they value your input, and never push or pressure. And if they start sexting too soon, you'll know all they want is to get into your pants, not into your heart.

5. **They're a straight shooter, in real life and on social media.** They're proud to show up with you online and off. They don't keep you a secret. They also don't use social media as a manipulative tool to make you jealous, insecure, or play games.

6. **They don't come on too strong.** They don't make grand romantic gestures or pronouncements in the first few dates like "I want to spend the rest of my life with you," or "I could see myself marrying you." Those are big red flags. Excessive flattery, attention, and compliments should also set off alarm bells. Someone who overpromises will most always underdeliver. And if they say "I want to take care of you" on the first date, they're full of shit, most likely a narcissist, and have no intention of making good on their offer.

7. **They aren't afraid of intimacy.** They can get close and not freak out. When things get serious, they don't run. Instead, they step up. And if they can't step up, they bow out gracefully and proactively.

Your right person might not be around the corner; they might be light years away, or right in front of your face the whole time, but just not ready. So don't curse the universe; trust it instead. Because when you do meet your person, *you* will have the right stuff to know if they're right for you.

# NINE

# I DATED
# LORD VOLDEMORT

*Just when the caterpillar thought the world
was over, it became a butterfly.*

—English proverb

**T**he cruel reality of my relationship life was this: I ended the right ones when I thought I had all the time in the world, and stayed with the wrong ones when I thought time was running out.

This was never more the case than when I dated a guy I nicknamed Lord Voldemort, the evil character from the Harry Potter series: a character so malevolent you can't even utter his name. Unlike J. K. Rowling's Voldemort, though, my version was handsome, charming, five-minutes divorced, and completely unavailable.

In other words, he was just my type.

We went out for a year and a half, during which I never stopped hoping my love could fix him, and his love could fix everything for me. He was my last hope before my eggs dried up.

He wasn't a bad guy, and far from evil; he was just bad for me. Nonetheless, I made him my project, because I had my own project: to get married and pregnant. I was determined, even if it meant putting up with a guy I had no business dating in the first place. Actually, *he* shouldn't have been dating in the first place. It was way too soon, he was too raw, and I doubt he could've been a boyfriend to anyone. By the time I realized this, though, I was in too deep.

Dating him was death by a thousand cuts. I never knew where I stood, and lived and died waiting for reassurance from him. Instead, there were mixed messages and silence. I knew it wasn't healthy; I knew I needed to break up with him, but I couldn't bring myself to do it. I had too much on the line.

The final blow came while on a "friend fix-up." My friend Jonathan wanted me to meet his associate Jodi, a fellow single gal who had gone to my high school and was as nice as can be. He thought we'd make good friends. Since you can never have enough running buddies when you're single, I was more than happy to meet her.

As Jodi and I were getting to know each other, the subject of boyfriends came up. I began telling her about my on-again, off-again relationship with Lord Voldemort, and as I was giving her the details, the color drained from her face. Without saying another word, she pulled out her phone and showed me a text thread between them. Turns out my boyfriend Lord Voldemort had a secret online dating life. When this came to light, I excused myself to the ladies' room to hyperventilate.

Talk about divine intervention. What I couldn't do myself, again the universe (and Jodi) did for me. It was the final straw that broke the camel's back. It also broke me.

For weeks, I couldn't eat, sleep, work, or stop crying. I couldn't even say his name. Along with not being able to function, I lost a ton of weight, my hair fell out, and the anti-anxiety drug Ativan became my BFF.

As I bottomed out, my new friend Jodi launched into action. I hardly knew her, but she became like my AA sponsor, calling me daily, urging me to stay strong, and keeping me from falling off the wagon. I stayed away from Voldemort, which wasn't easy. So many times I wanted to call him, but the deal was, if I felt weak and was tempted to dial his number, I would dial Jodi's instead.

My other "sponsor" was Tom, my male BFF, who had been a one-man safe haven for me during my single years. His importance in my life cannot be understated. He was the brother I never had, and provided unconditional support for me after every breakup. I introduced him to Jodi, and they both came to my rescue.

When Jodi and Tom weren't lecturing me about self-worth and admonishing me for undervaluing myself, they were nursing me back to health with medical marijuana. I say "medical" because back when it was still illegal in California, you had to have a doctor's note to buy it. The fact was, I was in crisis, and weed was just what the doctor ordered.

With their help, I found just enough self-worth and mustered up enough discipline to get myself back on track and stay there. By "discipline," I mean that I went full trainer on myself. The Lord Voldemort experience brought me to my knees, but it also brought me to my senses. It was time to get myself into emotional shape.

**The Lord Voldemort experience brought me to my knees, but it also brought me to my senses.**

There was a pattern to my dating life that I was able to track back to my parents. Their chaos and instability were familiar to me, and I was recreating it in my adult relationships. It was the ultimate self-sabotage. I wanted a relationship, but couldn't blame the guy when it didn't work out. The blame was on me for picking (or sticking with) the wrong guy to begin with.

## ATTACHMENT THEORY TO THE RESCUE

Years later, when I learned about attachment theory, everything made sense. Attachment theory is a branch of psychology originated in the 1950s and 1960s, based on research conducted by John Bowlby and Mary Ainsworth.[17] The the-

---

17   Courtney E. Ackerman, "What Is Attachment Theory? Bowlby's 4 Stages Explained," *Positive Psychology*, April 27, 2018, https://positivepsychology.com/attachment-theory/.

ory explains how people build lasting emotional connections based on their upbringing and childhood. According to attachment theory, the availability of a caregiver or parent, and the quality of care or bond you get with them as a child, impacts future romantic bonds and informs relationships as an adult. Simply put, the way you were loved or saw love as a child is how you'll experience and demonstrate love as an adult.

Attachment theory is the foundation for every interaction you have, not just love. It informs all of your relationships, friendships, and business partnerships.

Based on decades of research, psychologists have identified four primary attachment styles:

- **Secure:** People with secure style are satisfied with their relationships and feel secure and connected to their partners without feeling the need to be together all the time. These relationships are likely to feature honesty, support, independence, and deep emotional connections.

- **Anxious:** Anxious style partners may feel desperate for love or affection and feel that their partner must "complete" them or fix their problems. While they long for safety and security, they may also push their partner away rather than invite them in. Anxious attachment can include being clingy, demanding, jealous, or easily upset by small issues.

- **Avoidant:** People with this attachment style generally keep their distance from others. They may feel that they don't need human connection to survive or thrive and insist on maintaining their independence and isolation from others.

- **Fearful-Avoidant (or Disorganized):** Manifesting as ambivalence rather than isolating, people with fearful-avoidant style try to avoid their feelings so as not to get overwhelmed by them. They often fear getting hurt.

I immediately identified myself as a little of all four. I could get close, but feared getting hurt, so I kept my heart safe by keeping an arm's distance. Not a sustainable way to date, let alone function in a relationship.

If you identify with any of this, ask yourself: What's the source of my pain? What needs fixing? Where did I pick up these habits? What old trauma keeps me suffering?

Be real, be honest, be brave, and don't be afraid to ask for help. Don't take old wounds, grief, or anger into your next relationship or future. Do whatever it takes to heal and be free.

Once your wound has healed and a scab has formed, don't pick at it. It doesn't matter if it's a broken heart, a bruised ego, or a wounded psyche—don't touch it.

**Once your wound has healed and a scab has formed, don't pick at it.**

Don't text, call, communicate, have sex with, or stalk your ex on social media. I've drunk-texted, dialed in moments of weakness, and hooked up after breaking up. All of this picked the scab because it undermined my progress and prolonged my pain.

## Purge Your Ex Like a Pro

To keep from picking the scab after a breakup I created "The Ex Purge," a list of hardcore, tough-love breakup tips that are guaranteed to heal your heart and return you to badass status.

1.  After a breakup, let yourself be broken and allow yourself to grieve. Cry all day and night, as hard and long as you want. Don't put a timetable on this. Get every bit of grief and sadness out of your system. When you've gone a day without crying, get to work.

2.  Immediately purge all traces of your ex, including photos, gifts, or other sentimental items. If you can't part with them entirely, at least put them away until you're stronger. You'll know you're healed when these items don't trigger you or your memories.

3.  Wash all sheets, towels, blankets, clothes, or anything else that smells of your ex. Burn sage around your home to get the last remaining bad energy out.

4. Delete your ex from your contacts. Don't look at their name, phone number or email address. Just seeing their contact info can be a trigger. Also, stay away from your mutual friends for a while so you won't be tempted to ask questions or get updates on your ex.

5. Unfollow or mute—don't block—your ex on social media. You don't want to look at their activity, but you do want them to see you moving on.

6. Every day for a week, handwrite a full page of stream-of-conscious thoughts on a pad of paper. Curse, rant, vent, and list every unattractive thing about your ex. Dump all your thoughts on the page. Make sure to include *positive* self-affirmations about yourself too (you want to stay empowered, not victimized). Don't stop till you reach the bottom. Don't go back and re-read, don't edit for spelling or grammar. When you're done, tear it out, crumple it up, and throw it away.

7. Start a meditation practice ASAP. I highly recommend Mindfulness-Based Stress Reduction (MBSR; see box at the end of the chapter) with some extra-creative visualization and self-empowerment thrown in.

8. If you aren't exercising already, start with 20 minutes a day, even if it's just a brisk walk. Get your heart rate up long enough to break a sweat. Your endorphins will expedite the healing process.

9. Practice self-care and pampering. Get massages, facials, mani-pedis, take naps, etc. Indulge yourself with extra kindness and comfort.

10. See a therapist for three to six months, and that's it. Get off the couch as soon as possible so you can put your new skills to work.

11. Enlist your friends and family to keep you accountable and on track. Ask them to check in, hang out, and help keep your mind off your ex.

12. Limit your time talking about your ex or breakup. The more you talk about it, the more life and power you give it.

13. Stop romanticizing your ex. Focus on the negatives to remind yourself why it didn't work out.

*continued*

**14.** For the same reasons I'm not in favor of having sex too soon after a breakup, I'm also not in favor of dating too soon after a breakup. It can backfire and send you running back to your ex. Better to heal first. You wouldn't walk with a broken leg, so don't date with a broken heart.

**15.** Be disciplined and stay the course. A better person is out there for you, and a better *you* is coming.

The final touch of The Ex Purge is resisting the temptation to undo it all. If you're serious about moving forward and putting the past behind you, you've got to be ruthless. Don't pick the scab, don't touch the wound, don't look back. It will heal nicely, and so will you.

—

In the years after Lord Voldemort I would have more relationships (and breakups), but after each one, I got smarter. I became extra careful with my heart, and extra vigilant with to whom I gave it. I swore to myself I would never give that much power to a man again, and I've kept my promise.

If someone had told me back then that one day I'd thank Lord Voldemort, I would've said they were crazy. But crazily enough, I did thank him. He gave me the impetus to do much-needed healing work, and when I finally healed, I was able to be his friend. Turns out he's not Lord Voldemort after all and not one bit evil. He's a good guy, with a good heart, who needed a little healing himself.

# TEST-DRIVEN TAKEAWAYS

As mentioned in the preceding tips, I highly recommend starting a meditation practice, which might be the best tip of all. When your heart is heavy and head is noisy, meditation quiets, calms, and centers you. I practice MBSR (Mindfulness-Based Stress Reduction) with some extra creative visualization and self-empowerment thrown in. Here's how to start:

# Meditate Like a Pro

- Give yourself 10 minutes a day to sit quietly. Close your eyes, breathe slowly and deeply, and scan your body, releasing areas of tension.
- Think of things that you're grateful for.
- Practice forgiveness and releasing anger by seeing your ex get into a hot air balloon. Untie the ropes and let them fly away. Send them off with love.
- Create some empowering words or sentences and see them on a black background in white type and repeat them a few times: "I am fully healed," "I am powerful," "I release my anger," "I am loved."
- In your mind's eye, visualize moving forward, accomplishing goals, and feeling great.

**TEN**

# KEEP YOUR LEGS OPEN AND YOUR FINGERS CROSSED

*The best time to plant a tree was 20 years ago.*
*The second best is now.*

—Chinese proverb

After Lord Voldemort, shit got real. No more wasting time, no more Westward Ho. The late bloomer in me had had enough and was ready to take destiny into her own hands.

My clock was ticking louder than ever, and my desire to get married and have kids was only getting more urgent. With few options on the table, I did what any crazy, fearless, gutsy, single woman of a certain age would do: I decided to get pregnant on my own.

This was my midlife crisis. When most people are marking their midlife crises with fast cars, plastic surgery, divorce, or affairs with people half their age, I was looking to get knocked up.

A woman's fertility usually starts declining at 35, and I was 43. Time was not on my side. To remind me, my gynecologist tapped his watch and said that if I wanted to get pregnant, I'd have to get on the stick. But whose stick? I was stone-cold single, with no boyfriend, husband, friend with benefits, or booty call. It was bad enough I couldn't find anyone to marry me; now I had to find someone to make a baby with me.

Being a single mother by choice was not my dream. I did not grow up thinking, "I want to be a single mother one day!"—but I had no choice. If I wanted a kid, it was now or never. So with no immediate prospects to help me conceive—and no time to freeze my eggs either—I went right to getting pregnant with donor sperm.

## ALL THAT JIZZ

After doing some quick research, I located an online cryobank, searched through the catalogue of young, virile donors, and found the sperm of my dreams: high IQ, decent looking, good swimmers, few to no other donor babies, and no history of mental wackiness (which I already have enough of in my own family). It was like online dating for baby daddies, but without the paradox of choice. I knew exactly what I wanted.

Just to be sure, though, I had a sperm donor selection party with my closest girlfriends to help me decide. We sat around drinking wine and passing the donor bios around in a circle until we chose a winner: Donor #3486. He was Jewish, educated, and looked sort of like me. He'd be the lucky sperm. I wouldn't have to date or marry him; I just had to buy him to make him mine and he couldn't refuse. It was the easiest relationship I'd ever have.

The donor selection process is so much like online dating that you have to remember you're *not* dating these guys, you're just using them for conception. The next day, I ordered a few vials and got to work. And by work, I mean the ensuing visits to the fertility doctor, plus follow-up ultrasounds and blood tests. On top of that were Chinese acupuncture treatments, plus hours scouring Craigslist for cheap fertility drugs and nutritional supplements.

On my first insemination, I got pregnant. And cocky. I was giving myself high-fives for getting it done in one shot, but two weeks later, I found out it was a chemical pregnancy, and it didn't last. Always the competitor, defeat only made me go harder —and spend more money.

This mission would end up costing me thousands of dollars—a hardship on a personal trainer's income—but I did it anyway because I wanted a baby. Let me break it down for you. Just to get in the door and meet with a doctor for an initial fertility consultation and labs costs $450. Each vial of sperm costs about $800–$1,000, then $275 to ship the sperm FedEx, and about $400 for each insemination. Intrauterine inseminations (IUIs) are the easiest, cheapest, and least invasive—and you pray it works, otherwise you have to bring in the big guns of in vitro fertilization (IVF). IVF costs about $30,000 per cycle, which includes labs, embryology, and medications.

It should be mentioned that this was all happening during the Great Recession of 2008. I didn't even realize we were in a financial crisis because I was so focused on baby-making. At a time when I should've been safeguarding every penny I ended up draining my savings, racking up enormous debt, ruining my credit, and putting myself into bad financial straits. I was looking at hundreds and hundreds of hours training clients to pay it all back, an impossible task. The biggest hardship, though, was having to lie about the whole thing to my highly disapproving parents.

When I first broke the news to my parents that I was attempting to have a baby on my own, I expected a standing ovation; instead I received universal condemnation. They called me selfish and irresponsible, and refused to support me. I knew right then I'd have to keep it a secret, and I did. I broke the 11th Commandment of not lying to my father. He made me swear that I wouldn't go through with it, but I secretly stayed on course, full steam ahead. Unbeknownst to them I was getting pricked, probed, and poked every time I ovulated. The only thing I couldn't hide was my emotional state, which was fragile and subject to mood swings and crying jags (thanks, fertility drugs!).

When my mother and I went to see the 2009 animated movie *Up*, I was completely blindsided by the scene where the main character Carl Fredricksen and his wife Ellie suffer a miscarriage, then find out she's unable to have children. I started sobbing. Hard. I was bawling so hard and loud, my mother looked at me like I was a crazy person and asked, "Why are you crying? It's a cartoon."

Little did she know I was hopped up on hormones and going through my own live-action fertility drama.

## WORK . . . THAT OTHER FOUR-LETTER WORD

As the months went on, "work" also meant conceiving by any means necessary, not just in a doctor's office. Work meant having timed intercourse with "known" donors. These donors appeared in the form of good Samaritans or old flames, who offered me their seed with no strings attached. My fertility window was closing fast, so all options were on the table: inseminations in the stirrups or sex the old-fashioned way. Known or unknown sperm—it didn't matter, whatever got me pregnant first. My motto was "Keep your legs open and your fingers crossed."

> **My fertility window was closing fast, so all options were on the table: inseminations in the stirrups or sex the old-fashioned way.**

One of the good Samaritans who stepped up during this time was a guy from college who found me on JDate. We started chatting, and after a few exchanges, I told him about my baby quest. He didn't flinch; in fact, he signed up. Instead of love-bombing me he "baby-bombed" me, with promises of helping me conceive, pay for, and raise my child. He was all-in for more than just sperm. He wanted to be my baby daddy.

For a few weeks we tried to "date" as I tried to get pregnant, which was weird, but I didn't care: He was going to make my dream come true.

I put all my eggs in his basket, so to speak. He was someone I knew, he had money, and came from a good family—and then one day out of the blue, he abruptly changed his mind and dropped me like a hot potato.

I'll spare you the tears and devastation part and just tell you that I got back in the saddle (and stirrups) as fast as I could. This guy was the exception, but in my experience, if you tell a guy you're trying to get pregnant *not with his sperm*, he'll love you, be there for you, and support you in every way (except financially). If it's not going to be his kid, he's good to go. He'll have sex with you all day long, just as long as he doesn't have to pay for the kid or raise it.

Not long after the baby-bomber, I met a guy who turned into a real boyfriend that I cared for deeply. We dated for about a year, but despite his Michael Phelps–quality swimmers, good heart, and best intentions, he couldn't knock me up to save my life.

At this point, sex started feeling like a chore. Whenever I ovulated, I'd launch into action. I'd go on fuck binges, having as much sex as I could in a 48-hour period—which sounds like a hell of a great time, but it was actually just plain hell. I never thought of sex as drudgery, but it is when you're trying to conceive. "Work" became interchangeable with that other four-letter word.

Meanwhile, time was ticking, and I wasn't getting any younger.

Nor was I getting pregnant, and nothing seemed to help—not drugs, acupuncture, or even a devoted boyfriend. The mission dragged on, and I was losing hope. My relationship was also losing hope, so we parted ways and I went back to being single again, with a few unused vials of sperm from Donor #3486 in my back pocket.

**I never thought of sex as drudgery, but it is when you're trying to conceive.**

I felt very alone. The baby-making process can test even the strongest of couples, but when you're single, you're never more on your own. I never feel sorry for myself, but this experience gave me plenty to pity. Like getting ultrasounds without anyone to hold my hand or sitting alone in my fertility doctor's waiting room surrounded by loving couples. I remember seeing a trans couple there, which made me smile and sad at the same time. Even they could make a baby.

Then there's having to give yourself hormone shots in your butt without a partner to help. I administered all of my own shots, but on occasion my friend Tobey would give me a hand. I'd pull my pants down, lean over the dining room table, and she'd shoot me in the ass with a filled syringe. This was my standing ovation, I guess.

The saddest part always were the calls I'd get from my doctor with pregnancy results. It was always bad news, I always cried, and there was always no one to hug me after I hung up.

I knew my eggs were probably past their expiration date, and I was running out of money, but I wasn't ready to give up. I still had some hope left in the form of my then 20-year-old cousin, Callie, who valiantly donated her eggs to me. As a Hail Mary, I flew her to LA from Florida, moved her in with me, got her set up with my doctor, bought the drugs, and taught her how to give herself shots. Two weeks later we retrieved a bunch of nice, healthy eggs, and I was thrilled. We mixed her eggs with sperm from Donor #3486 and waited the requisite three days for the eggs to fertilize.

By day five, a couple of blastocysts had formed (the stage at which embryos are implanted), and I was even more thrilled. Callie's work was done, so I sent her back to Florida and scheduled my embryo transfer.

I went back to the doctor for the procedure, bringing my friend Laurie along for moral support (at this point these procedures had become noneventful, almost rote, but this was my last hurrah). Like a devoted husband, Laurie brought me a bouquet of flowers and stood by my side as the embryos were implanted. I went home and waited another dreaded two weeks for results. Even with my fingers crossed, legs open, and embryos made from 20-year-old eggs trying to hatch inside me, I still couldn't get pregnant.

## NEXT STOP, SELF-LOATHINGVILLE

So after nearly four years, six IUIs, three rounds of IVF, two donor egg transfers, days of waiting time, and too much timed intercourse to remember, I ended my quest. I had moved heaven and earth, put my body through hell, and come up empty. And to make matters worse, I still wasn't even close to getting married. By the time all was said and done, I was 47. Stupid me for thinking I had all the time in the world, and that my fertility would last forever.

I hit another kind of bottom with this failure, but I had to press on. Questioning why I failed would've sent me down a dark spiral of self-recriminations: Was it karma for waiting too long? Payback for bad decisions? Or was it the late bloomer striking again? I'd known failure before, but the failure to conceive was next-level: talk about all your past mistakes coming back to smack you in the face (or shoot you in the ass, in my case).

In an effort to stop myself from going to Self-Loathingville, I instead put the experience behind me as quickly as I could. I didn't seek out therapy, join a support group, or employ any extraordinary measures to help me get over the disappointment, I just forged ahead with my life, sans baby or husband.

What helped me was the pride I got from embarking on the mission in the first place. I have to acknowledge the Herculean task it was and give myself credit. I may have failed in the attempt to make a baby—but I would've been a failure had I not tried.

Project Baby wasn't a success, but I'm not sorry I did it, nor do I have regrets (although I do have many regrets about not doing it sooner). Not being able to have kids does get to me sometimes. Like when I see my friends' children or grandchildren on social media. It tugs at my heart, then it warms my heart. I'm happy for them, and I'm happy for me. I went for it, gave it my all, put every-thing on the line—and in doing so, it showed me what I was made of. I can give myself those high-fives now.

After my baby journey came to an end, I would tell myself: *When one door closes, another one opens.* If motherhood wasn't in the cards, at least a real rela-tionship could be, or maybe even marriage one day. And some dating doors did open, but nothing lasted, and that was OK, because I wasn't in such a hurry anymore. I could slow down, take a breath, and just be. I also stopped watching the clock, and that, more than anything, allowed me to exhale.

Trying to get pregnant was exactly the thing I needed. I became more aware of time, more respectful of my body, and more appreciative of money (spending a fortune you don't have on fertility procedures, drugs, sperm, and labs can do that).

Another unintended benefit of my pregnancy quest was the direct impact it had on my dating life. Now that I was back on the market, things would be dif-ferent. Post-fertility dating would mean no more forcing square pegs into round holes and cutting bait faster when things weren't working out. As ready as I was to open a new door, life would make me wait again.

# TEST-DRIVEN TAKEAWAY

Single ladies of child-bearing age who are reading this: If you want kids one day, run to your nearest fertility doctor and freeze your eggs NOW. Or if you're a mother, sister, or friend of a single woman who's of child-bearing age, drive them yourself! If it's crunch time and your eggs are "aging out" (ouch!), find some jizz and go knock yourself up. The point is not to wait. You can get married at any age; but you can't get pregnant with your own eggs at any age. While you're contemplating all this, be aware of what's happening to women's rights, and stay informed about reproductive laws in your state. Keep your legs open, and I'll keep my fingers crossed.

# ELEVEN

# THE BLOOM IS
# OFF THE ROSE

*Love enters later in life through the cracks*
*left by the first heartbreak.*

—D. Biswas

A fter so many doors had closed, it was pure delight when a door opened in the spring of 2012, less than a year before I turned 50. How serendipitous! Right before I become an old maid, I meet someone! Thank you, universe, for delivering Mr. Right and saving me from spinsterhood!

This open door came in the form of a divorced dad, whom I had known years earlier through mutual friends. Turns out he had gotten divorced, and much to my surprise was friends with my bookie, who fixed us up.

He checked off all the boxes: good chemistry, compatible, geographically desirable, and in alignment politically, culturally, and otherwise. Plus, he had been divorced long enough for me to feel it was safe to date him. Everything about him—the past connection and my bookie's intervention—said he was The One. With everything I had been through, it felt like destiny.

Things were going swimmingly for the first three months, but in month 4, something telling happened. While out to dinner we ran into some friends, and it was at that moment I detected some hesitance from him. When my friend playfully asked if we were boyfriend and girlfriend, The One looked at me blankly, not offering an automatic, emphatic "yes." So I shrugged and said, "I think so?" with a question mark and an awkward laugh.

He was a fairly reserved guy to begin with, so I chalked it up to shyness, put it out of my mind, and kept on dating him. My hope was that if he had any trepidation, he'd work through it and eventually realize I was The One for him.

At the six-month point, we were well into a relationship. We introduced each other to our friends and broke the Yom Kippur fast together with our families, but we still hadn't said "I love you" to each other. This didn't occur to me until my BFFs Tom and Jodi brought it to my attention. It troubled them, so it troubled me. At six months in, you should probably know if you love someone, so upon their urging I decided to find out what the holdup was.

## WE NEED TO TALK (CUE THEME TO *JAWS*)

It was a warm Sunday, a couple of days before the November 2012 presidential election, when I had him over to chat. I had no doubt the outcome would be positive: I'd get my answer, and we'd keep on dating. Besides, I was wearing cut-off Levi's shorts and looked cute. Who's going to dump me when I'm wearing cut-off shorts? I was confident I'd prove my friends wrong and that he loved me, but was just too shy to say it.

He sat down and we proceeded to have "The Talk": "Where are we going, what do you want, why haven't we said 'I love you,' at six months you should know," blah, blah, blah. As the conversation wore on, it became painfully clear that although he enjoyed being with me, I wasn't The One, nor was he looking for The One.

I'll never forget his words to me: "Love isn't a priority for me right now." They were words I didn't want to hear, but I heard them loud and clear. As a consolation, he said: "Let's just keep going and see what happens." I understood this as an option to hang in for an indeterminate amount of time while he figured out if it was love or not. Would I be game?

I felt like a contestant on the old game show *Let's Make A Deal*, where host Monty Hall would ask: "Would you rather have what's behind Door #2 or what's in the box?" Both offerings were unknown, and only one was the prize.

I was an exemplary girlfriend. I gave him space and let him lead. I wasn't too clingy or needy, and made zero demands. I answered texts, but never initiated them. If there was an award for Chill Girlfriend of the Year, I would've won it.

But here I was, facing that new door, not sure if it was open, closing, or just being kept ajar depending on what I wanted. And that was part of the problem. I never told him what I really wanted because I was afraid of scaring him off.

My stomach was in knots, my heart was in my throat, and my head was spinning with options. I could've laid out a thousand reasons to love me, but instead, I took a deep breath and said:

"I'm sorry, but this is as good as it's going to get. I can't be any more wonderful than I am right now, and if you don't love me now, you're never going to love me."

I threw down the gauntlet, after which came a long, awkward silence. We both waited for the other to decide: either go forward or end it. He shed a few tears, told me he cared about me (which I believed since I knew him to be an honest, good person), but we ended up not wanting to go forward.

Mr. Love Isn't a Priority didn't want to make me a priority, so I pulled the ripcord and proactively ended it right there and then—an act of defiance and self-respect that surprised even me.

**I didn't want to be someone's *maybe or later.*** I was quickly reminded of the vow I made to myself after Lord Voldemort: There'd be no more waiting to be loved, appreciated, and cherished. There'd be no more half-hearted, one-foot-in, semi-availability, and no more being put on the backburner. I didn't want to be someone's *maybe* or *later*. If a serious relationship was what I really wanted, if a guy with conviction was what I needed, then I needed to say it. So I said it, and he heard me loud and clear.

I repeated silently to myself: *I know who I am. I know what I've got*, while I sat there, half-beaming with pride inside, half-dying inside. I also repeated silently to myself: *his loss, my gain*, and by gain, I meant my dignity and self-esteem. I had promised myself years earlier that no man would ever kill my soul again, and I wasn't about to go back on my word.

Despite the tough talk, though, the whole thing left me in ruins. I called him a week later hoping for some closure (really, a change of heart), anything to make me feel better, but no such luck. He didn't fight for me, and that was all the closure I needed.

I was a seasoned pro at breakups; I knew the drill, yet I was a sobbing mess in the weeks after. I cried throughout November and was numb and depressed throughout much of December. Nothing felt good, tasted good, sounded good. Christmas and New Year's were a blur. It all sucked.

I thought I had played this one right, but like with so many others, it ended up a DNF (track and field term for "Did Not Finish").

## POST-BREAKUP BLUES

Many times after a breakup I'd get philosophical, and this was no exception. I told myself there was a bigger plan, that meeting him was a stepping-stone to something greater. This thinking saved me many times in the past, and it saved me again in that moment.

This quote from the blogger and life coach known as the Angry Therapist summed up my feelings: "Life doesn't always introduce you to the people you want to meet. Sometimes, life puts you in touch with the people you need to meet to help you, to hurt you, to leave you, to love you, and to gradually strengthen you into the person you were meant to become."[18]

---

18   See the Angry Therapist's website at https://www.theangrytherapist.com.

I had experienced breakup pain with Lord Voldemort, but this pain was different because the stakes were so much higher. I was about to turn 50, a scary milestone. When you're single in your 30s, no one thinks anything of it. When you're single in your 40s, people might start to wonder. But when you're 50 or over and still single? People talk.

Even though as a society, we've come a long way and have made great strides in how we view unmarried people, I still hear echoes from a time when it was considered abnormal *not* to be married, especially by a certain age. This narrative never stopped running through my mind—and was at a fever pitch as I was about to turn 50.

It was the perfect storm of despair: I wasn't married, couldn't get pregnant, couldn't make a relationship last, I was deep in debt, and my once-gratifying fitness career had grown stagnant. At almost 50, I was no longer young or fertile or desirable. The bloom was off the rose, as they say.

I wasn't a hot chick anymore. I was now officially an old maid, "a single woman regarded as too old for marriage."

# THE LATE-BLOOMING BRIDE
# GROWS SOME BALLS

*Train yourself to let go of everything you fear to lose.*

—Yoda

After breaking up with Mr. Love Isn't a Priority, I called a truce with myself and waved the white flag. I was done. Done with dating, done with relationships, done with marriage, done with hope.

Dating and relationships had become minefields, filled with danger at every turn, rejection and hurt lurking around every corner, potential heartbreak with each step. I wasn't sure I had it in me to tough it out anymore.

The truth is, falling in love takes balls. When you dare to love, you take your chances and throw caution to the wind. You open your heart, cross your fingers, leap, and hope not to die. I decided the whole thing was too death-defying and not for me. I wasn't afraid to love, I was afraid of not being loved back.

Love should give you butterflies, not gastritis. Love should be euphoric, not anxiety-inducing. Love should make you high, but the only high I got was from the weed I smoked to calm my anxiety and gastritis.

I would meet someone and the questions would start: *I wonder if he's into me? I wonder if it will last? I wonder how he feels? I wonder if he'll call? I wonder if I'll ever stop wondering?*

As the relationship developed, so would a whole new set of questions: *What if we don't share the same goals? What if I'm honest and he thinks I'm too much? What if he finds out I'm not perfect?*

The questions I should've been asking myself were: *Where the hell was my self-worth? What happened to my personal code? Where was the confident woman I once knew and loved?* Nowhere to be found.

I gave dating my best shot. I hung in there. I went the distance. I hit it hard and left nothing on the field. Now, there was only one thing left to do:

Quit.

I quit wondering, worrying, and waiting to get married, and made peace with being single the rest of my life.

## HIT IT AND QUIT

Even though quitting went against everything I knew as an athlete, it was exactly the thing I had to do at that moment.

As it turns out, it wasn't really that hard. Once I released my death grip on marriage, suddenly all my boy problems went away. When I took marriage off the table I was liberated, no longer imprisoned by my hopes or chained to a goal that had become deadweight.

My job as a fitness pro and coach is to get people strong, but nowhere in any coaching manual does it say you can get strong by giving up. I discovered that little secret on my own. Quitting, I've realized, is as much a part of self-improvement as discipline and hard work.

I did what author Seth Godin calls "strategic quitting."[19]

---

19    Seth Godin, *The Dip: A Little Book That Teaches You When to Quit (and When to Stick)* (New York: Penguin/Portfolio, 2007).

Strategic quitting or smart quitting is when your current path isn't getting you toward your goal, so you cut your losses and turn your attention toward other productive pursuits. I quit because I wasn't making progress. I quit because dating was hurting more than helping. I quit because my self-esteem was taking too many hits.

I'd like to say making the decision to quit was brave, but it wasn't. My psyche just gave out, and so did my intrepid spirit.

As I've learned, quitting isn't a loser strategy, it's a smart move when you keep hitting walls, fail to get results, or lack the passion to keep grinding it out. When you surrender for the right reasons, you find strength in other areas; when you stop twisting yourself into pretzels to attain an all-or-nothing goal, you actually might attain it. When you walk away, whatever is lost is regained in power and pride.

Quitting released me. No more overthinking and overanalyzing, no more trying to decode someone's every move, no more deciphering texts, and no more dating drama. It even cured me of the chronic matrimania I had been suffering with for years.

I was free.

I followed novelist E. M. Forster's advice: "We must be willing to let go of the life we have planned, so as to have the life that is waiting for us."

I knew my current path wasn't getting me anywhere. My goal of getting married had become self-defeating, so I let go of the dream and turned it into a new dream of being happily single.

Here's the caveat: Even though I gave up on love, I never gave up on *loving myself*, which made all the difference.

My new dream of being happily single meant keeping my intrepid spirit, sense of adventure, and curiosity. I had survived the first 50 years without a partner, so why not just keep going?

At the same time I let marriage go, I let go of the stigma of being single. I decided

**Even though I gave up on love, I never gave up on *loving myself*, which made all the difference.**

I would no longer let it negatively impact me, define me, shame me, or keep me from living life on my own terms. In this moment I was reminded of Anaïs Nin's famous quote: "The day came when the risk to remain tight in a bud was more painful than the risk it took to bloom."

I had to risk blooming in a different way.

All the struggles I overcame to get to this point suddenly felt like a badge of honor, so I decided to channel my inner Carrie Bradshaw and wear it proudly. Hell, if I was going to be an old maid, I was going to make it look good.

## NO PITY PARTY FOR ME

Instead of having a pity party for my 50th birthday (like anyone in the depths of despair would've done), I threw myself a *party* party. I figured that since I was never going to have a wedding, this would be the next best thing. First, I designed invitations that superimposed my face onto the movie poster for *This Is 40*, except I changed it to *This Is 50*. Then I rented out a karaoke bar and invited all my friends, family, and half of Facebook—about 75 people, the size of a small wedding. The only thing missing was a chuppa and a rabbi.

The party was exactly the kind of wedding I would've wanted: lots of tequila, music, dancing, singing, and celebrating. I always gauge the success of a party by the level of hangover I have the next day, and this one didn't disappoint. It was the best splitting headache I ever had.

One of the things that made my party so memorable was one of my invitees from Facebook named Robby Scharf. Robby and I had gone to the same high school, grew up in the same town, and had mutual friends, but we had never met.

I first became acquainted with Robby in the days after my breakup with Mr. Love Isn't a Priority. Robby DM'd me about a mutual friend who was having relationship problems. He was concerned and wanted to know if I'd be interested in doing an intervention for this friend, but I was in no mood and feeling too sorry for myself to lend a hand. Even if Robby was trying to flirt or had ulterior motives, it would've fallen on deaf ears, since I was too numb to be charming. I thanked him for reaching out and commended him for being such a caring friend. I took note that he was a good guy, and after looking at his profile picture again, I made another note that he was cute.

Just as I was sending out my party invitations, my friend Graem from high school called to tell me she had just run into Robby at Samy's Camera in LA. She sang his praises and told me how nice he was (which confirmed what I already sensed). Her seal of approval was enough for me to want to invite him to my party.

I DM'd Robby for his email address and told him I was sending him something. Two weeks later, after not receiving anything, Robby circled back and DM'd me again. That's when I realized I had totally forgotten to send him his invite.

I was scatterbrained; he was persistent.

When he arrived at the party, I was mildly surprised. After all, we had never met and he didn't know anyone, but that didn't stop him from showing up—with a bottle of Veuve Clicquot champagne in hand, and the cute smile I remembered from Facebook. It was like the most normal thing in the world to see him there. I welcomed him into the party with a big hug, as if I had known him all my life. It was instant warmth.

After the hug, I handed him a tequila shot and lost track of him for the rest of the party—that is, until I spotted him sitting with my father. I was on stage singing karaoke like a drunken fool, and made another mental note: "He's chatting up my father. Smart."

## Quit Like a Pro

Research has shown that the human brain is hardwired to persist; and to make matters worse, it's been drilled into our collective psyche that quitting is for losers.

To help you overcome the shame and stigma of quitting, I've asked Dr. Stanley Robertson, "The Quit Doctor," to give us some tips.* He uses the acronym Q.U.I.T. to make them easy to remember:

- **Quit quickly.** This means letting go as soon as you realize the situation is no longer working or serving you. Identify the

*continued*

things that aren't going anywhere and release them as quickly as possible. Successful people do not hesitate; they quit fast and often.

- **Understand negative emotions.** Acknowledge the negative emotions associated with quitting, and release those too. We're so conditioned to be ashamed if we give up, that we get stuck and stay there. Because of the stigma associated with quitting, many people persist in unhappy situations. While it may be embarrassing to admit failure, the alternative is worse. So if you want to find happiness, just admit that disappointment is part of life and move on.

- **Initiate a new goal.** Many times we're reluctant to quit the things that are familiar, because humans don't like change. But you can't grow unless you leave some things behind and open yourself up to new options. In relationships, it means viewing your newfound freedom as an opportunity to explore new territory. Reframe risks as opportunities to succeed rather than paths to failure. If you want to be happier and experience better relationships, be willing to seek out new partners and set new goals.

- **Transform your behavior.** To successfully quit, you must also quit your past behaviors. After you quit a goal and create a new one, your behavior will have to transform to line up with your new objective. To make progress in a new direction, you can't keep doing the same things you were doing before. Replace old behaviors with new attitudes and more self-awareness.

*See Dr. Robertson's website at https://drstan4.wixsite.com/website-1.

# INTRODUCING THE
# LATE-BLOOMING GROOM

*It's never too late to become who you might've been.*

—every refrigerator magnet you've ever seen

I don't remember much of what happened at my birthday party, since I was three sheets to the wind, but I do remember the next morning in my hungover state getting a call from Robby asking me out on a date for the following Thursday night, which happened to be the night after Valentine's Day. This was good timing since I already had a blind date scheduled for Valentine's evening with another guy (I know it's crazy to have a blind date on Valentine's, but when you're 50 and still single, traditional rules don't apply). So Robby and I made a date for February 15.

Even though I was excited to see Robby, I went on my Valentine's blind date anyway, more as a courtesy to the family friend who fixed me up. He turned out to be a leather-jacket-wearing, Porsche-driving, too-cool-for-school talent manager, who upon paying the check and getting up from the table, pulled me into him for a kiss and stuck his tongue into my mouth without asking.

I recoiled in horror, which made the drive home super uncomfortable. I guess he wasn't too happy about it either because when we arrived at my apartment, he dropped me off in the middle of the street and drove away without saying goodbye.

## NICE GUY IN A PRIUS

The next night was Robby, who showed up to my front door with a bouquet of flowers, wearing a gingham shirt and sweater vest. Nothing too groovy, nothing too showy, just a nice guy in a Prius.

As we drove off to dinner, Robby gave me the evening's itinerary: sushi at his favorite spot, followed by gelato at another favorite spot. That's when the control freak in me came out.

*"Make a left!"*

He looked at me like I was insane, but I wasn't—I was a jaded and cynical dater who in a fit of paranoia wanted to stay close to home just in case things went south. Like the gentleman he was, Robby gave in, and we ended up having our first date at a restaurant within walking distance of my apartment.

Over the next few months, Robby didn't let my jadedness and cynicism dissuade him. I kept my control issues at bay, and we continued to date without incident.

The next date ideas were all his, including a day of coaching at Special Olympics at Santa Monica High School. Robby's been a coach for 36 years, and he wanted the outing to be part of our courtship. And I'm so glad he did, because I got to see his good soul at work. He is so beloved by all the athletes there, and I'm pretty sure that's when I fell in love with him too.

After Special Olympics practice was over, we proceeded to play tennis on the high school courts nearby. At one point during our match he made a great shot, and I gave him the finger. Which was to say, "You can date me, just don't ever beat me in sports."

As things moved along, we established a comfort level with each other that was unlike anything I had ever experienced. It felt mature and steady, accepting and safe. I could be me with him.

For as well as I thought I knew men, I didn't really know the male species. They're apparently very gassy (my married friends would later confirm this). So when Robby started ripping farts and burping around me, I knew it was love.

And I didn't have gastritis with him, which meant I was relaxed.

In so many of my past relationships, the guy drove with the brakes on. Not Robby. He drove with his foot firmly on the gas pedal and never rode the brakes. He was all in, and a million miles ahead of anyone I had ever dated. He called when he said he would, didn't text excessively, and made plans in advance. He was direct, showed up on time, held the car door open for me, and was impeccable with his word.

Oh, and he didn't need fixing. Incredibly, he had no visible mental or emotional problems, no neuroses or attachment issues. Plus, he was

**When Robby started ripping farts and burping around me, I knew it was love.**

humble! Dating Robby was like hitting a six-team parlay (a bet that combines multiple games for a higher payout).

No love-bomber here: This guy was so proper that around four months into our relationship, he actually asked me if it was OK to say, "I love you." I squealed, "Of course it's OK! I love you too!"

What also made Robby different was that he also had never been married, or even engaged. He was a late bloomer just like me. Unbelievably, I had found my male counterpart! He had no kids, divorce, or crazy ex, and just enough baggage to make things interesting. He was a fucking unicorn! On top of that he was a Gemini, a fellow air sign, and his Venus trined my Saturn—an auspicious sign of stability.

I assumed he'd been single for so long because he was in the music business (as a musician and a music executive), and those types rarely settle down (except for Charlie Watts of the Rolling Stones, who was married for more than 60 years). But it wasn't his profession that kept Robby single. He just wasn't in a hurry and hadn't found the right person—which actually sounded a lot like me.

I asked him a million times why he was single, figuring there *had* to be something wrong with him. I probed, dug, interrogated, and of course, asked him about his relationship with his mother (always a tell-tale sign). I came up with nothing. He was normal and loved his mother.

My detective work was sufficient. His story checked out.

Born in Newark, New Jersey, Robby came from a loving home, with loving parents, Edward and Frances Scharf, and two older sisters, Wendy (nine years older) and Judith (eight years older).

Growing up with two older sisters gave him an early education into what women liked and didn't like in men. He saw how men's actions caused his sisters' reactions, and with that knowledge, Robby developed extra sensitivity and compassion when it came to women. This exceptional ability, plus the rest of his great qualities, was apparent early on, and I didn't need Google to confirm it. He was the real deal.

Musically, he's for real, too. He's been playing since he was six years old, starting on piano and guitar, eventually moving to bass guitar. He went on to play professionally, performing as a kid with the band Longfellow, which featured a young Shaun Cassidy on lead vocals, then with some pretty big acts including: Brian Wilson, The Beach Boys, Jim Messina, Jan and Dean, Leslie Gore, Mark Lindsay, Bobby Rydell, The Coasters, Tommy Sands, The Pranks, and The Cowsills, with whom Robby's been performing for more than 30 years.

He's also been a music executive, and an artist manager with Pat Rains and Associates, who represented jazz and R&B greats like Al Jarreau, David Sanborn, Joe Sample, The Crusaders, Marcus Miller, Aimee Mann, Wendy and Lisa, Gino Vannelli, Vonda Shepard, Jon Brion, and Charm Farm.

With all this musical experience, Robby gave new meaning to the term "Rock Star Boyfriend."

## RIGHT TIME, RIGHT PERSON, RIGHT MIND

We've all heard "right time, wrong person, wrong time, right person" as a reason for things working out or not. What we don't hear is "right mind," which is just as important in the dating equation. All the planets could be aligned, but if you're not in the right mind, it'll be all for naught. Because to even recognize the right person, your head must be in the right place.

As I've said, the right person will make themselves known, and Robby did. They will communicate their interest and intentions, and they won't play games or make you guess. The right person tells you where they stand.

That's not to say that things don't change. People change. They fall out of love or decide they've had enough. Breakups and divorce happen every day. Sometimes, we don't know people at all. We've all heard stories of that "perfect" spouse we thought we knew who cheated, or that great guy who turned into a psycho. This is why we take things slow, watch out for red flags, and use our gut feelings and free will to guide us.

## I COULD FINALLY BE MYSELF

Robby was right person, right time, and I was in the right frame of mind to know it.

I knew because he didn't make me worry or wonder. I knew because I didn't need a bong hit to deal. I knew because I could be myself—fears, faults, flaws, and all.

Our courtship was beautifully uneventful, and I liked it that way. That's when I realized that real love, good love, isn't a minefield, and never should be.

Six months into our relationship, while hanging out at his downtown LA loft drinking wine, the topic of moving in came up. I was living in an apartment in Beverly Hills, and Robby suggested we shack up to save rent and avoid the long commute (which on a good day, was about 45 minutes). It made sense, but I declined.

I had perfected single life. I was finally in a healthy relationship with myself and didn't want to fuck it up. Plus, I didn't want to play house at 50 years old, nor did I want to move in with someone just to save money.

My heart started pounding and my stomach tightened. I could feel we were entering a dangerous area of discussion, and I wanted to pick my words carefully.

"No one's ever asked me to move in, and I'm beyond flattered, but"—as I took a big gulp of wine—"I have to say no. If I moved anywhere with anyone, I'd have to have a firm commitment first. Can I have some more wine, please?"

This wasn't an ultimatum or a veiled marriage hint, it was me declaring what I felt worthy of. I wasn't good at telling someone what I needed, and I was sweating bullets. I hated these types of conversations; no good ever came of them.

Many relationships for me had timed out at the six-month point, and having "The Talk" was always the kiss of death. I figured for sure he was going to break up with me. Marriage was always a deal-breaker, and I sensed it coming.

My life was already complete before I met Robby. I didn't *need* to get married at this point, but I dreaded the thought of saying goodbye. So I steeled myself for what was sure to be an imminent ending to this fairytale romance.

But right in the middle of this incredibly tense moment, he excused himself from the conversation and walked over to the office area of his loft. I couldn't see what he was doing, I could only hear him rummaging through a plastic bag.

"What are you doing over there?"

"None of your beeswax," he shot back.

He finally returned to where I was sitting frozen in fear. Then he did something weird and got down on one knee and asked me to close my eyes. Immediately, I thought: *Oh, that's so cute. He's giving me a Cracker Jack placeholder ring, or some plastic crap from the last music convention he attended.*

Whatever it was, he slipped it on my *right*-hand ring finger.

"Wrong finger."

"Oops," said the guy who had never proposed to anyone. He quickly corrected himself and put it on my left ring finger and told me to open my eyes.

I opened my eyes to a ring, but it wasn't from a Cracker Jack box. It was a very delicate platinum diamond ring, very old like an heirloom.

"Will you marry me?" he asked.

I looked at the ring, at him, back at the ring again. I had never heard those words before. I didn't believe him, in fact, I thought it was one big joke.

"Shut the fuck up."

I looked at the ring curiously, thinking, *What's this strange thing on my finger?*

"It was my mother's. When she died, I was given a bag of her valuables, and this was in it."

A very long pause followed as my automatic breakup alert system activated.

"We don't have to do this," I said. "We can just keep dating, just keep going like we're going." I didn't want to ruin a good thing by inserting marriage into it, so I tried to get out of it.

He shook his head, not taking no for an answer. "I don't want you to spend another minute not knowing that I want to spend the rest of my life with you."

I looked around the room to see if I was on *Candid Camera* or if I was getting punk'd.

He asked again, "Will you marry me?"

I looked at him down on his knee, with an expression that was as genuine and loving as I've ever seen on a man's face. He was for real, and this was no *Candid Camera*. The decision was made. He won me over.

"OK, yes! Let's do it!"

The first person I called was my mom. I wanted to give her the good news first.

ME: Ma, guess what! I'm engaged!

MOM: With what?

That should tell you how much marriage was on anyone's minds.

We were done being single. I had never been asked, and he had never asked. It was a first for us both. It was like we blossomed at the same time.

## TEST-DRIVEN TAKEAWAYS

And now a word from our late-blooming groom, Robby, with some takeaways for the guys:

> As I hit my 30s, 40s, and 50s, I don't ever remember worrying about whether I would ever get married. I figured if it was "meant to be," it'll happen (and it did!). So do yourself a favor and stop

worrying. If you're serious about wanting to meet someone, be intentional, be positive, and keep the faith. If you want it, it can happen (but worrying won't make it happen any faster).

In every relationship I've had, whether it was someone new or someone I was seeing for a while, if I sensed it wasn't progressing or going where I wanted it to go, I'd get really honest with myself and choose to either work on it to make it better or end it. Life's too short to waste on someone who's not giving you what you want. There are too many other quality people out there who are ready to meet you. The question is, are you ready to meet them?

Enhance your chances by keeping these things in mind:

- Don't equate having great sex with someone with being in love. While having great sex is important in a relationship, if it becomes the main (or only) thing that connects you, the relationship won't succeed.

- If you find yourself constantly attracted to a specific type, and for whatever reason those relationships don't work out, it's time to start dating against type. Opening your mind might just open you up to a new relationship.

- Venture out of your comfort zone to meet new people, in new environments. Change up your routine, shop at different stores, and expand your sphere of activity.

- Guys, if you're on a blind date, whether it's a drink or a meal, pick up the check. Even if you never see your date again, at least she won't be left with the impression that you were cheap.

- The Roman philosopher Seneca once said that "Luck is what happens when preparation meets opportunity." Love is luck, but it's also preparation; meaning, if you want to attract someone, you've got to be attractive. So put some effort into your appearance, be well-groomed, and stay on top of your health and wellness.

# A BRIDE 51 YEARS
# IN THE MAKING

*You're never too old to set another goal or*
*dream a new dream.*

—attributed to motivational speaker Les Brown

Ten months later, Robby and I got married in what felt like a graduation ceremony of sorts. I had conquered singledom and tied the knot, something I never thought I could accomplish.

Taking my vows felt like an oath to myself, as much as they were an oath to Robby. It was my call to action, an athletic competition that I had trained for all my life. Up until that moment I was still playing in the minors, and suddenly, I get called up to the majors. I had to accept. I was ready for the big leagues, and ready to be someone's partner and wife and teammate.

I didn't get a signing bonus or a Graduation of Single Life diploma, but I did get a beautiful wedding at the Lakeside Golf Club in Los Angeles with all the bells and whistles, including six bridesmaids and groomsmen, chuppa holders, a

band, DJ, and tequila shots for our 200 guests. I made sure to include my friend
Jodi as bridesmaid (the one who came to my rescue during the Lord Voldemort
days), and I made my friend Tom a "bridesman." Our party favors were shot
glasses on which "L'Chaim Motherfuckers!" was printed in Hebrew-type font.

My wedding dress was my "something borrowed": a one-of-a-kind beaded
and sequined vintage creation designed by legendary TV costume designer Bob
Mackie back in the 1970s for my stepmother, actress Suzanne Charny. She wore
it for her second marriage (my dad is her third husband), and it was stored in a
box until I brought it back to life.

For entertainment, we had a bagpiper, honoring my mother's roots. To honor
Robby's rock roots we had the famous Cowsill family, Shaun Cassidy, Vicki
Peterson, and Bill Mumy performing in an all-star jam. I even took secret drum
lessons three months prior to the wedding and surprised Robby when I joined
the band to play "I'll Be Good to You" by the Brothers Johnson.

No stone was unturned, no detail spared. This is what happens when you
have 51 years to prepare for your wedding. In between my blind dates, bikini
waxes, and breakups, I planned every detail of my wedding. Every. Last. Detail.

For years, I saw it in my mind's eye, visualizing it in all its glory. I saw my
walk down the aisle, and my choreographed first dance to the little-known
Earth, Wind & Fire song "Side by Side." I just didn't know who the groom
was. I planned for years, dreaming of the impossible. I made mental notes
from other weddings, and filed it away in the "Oh well, a girl can dream, can't
she?" file.

Same for my wedding vows. I couldn't plan them, but I often wondered over
the years what I would say. When it was finally my turn I went into full copywriter
mode, treating my vows like a real writing assignment: I familiarized myself with
the product, did market research, identified my target audience, and got to work.
It was like the biggest freelance job I had ever gotten, and the client was me.

*As a freelance writer, I've written all kinds of things: from copy
to content, branding to blogging, screenplays to social media,
but I've never written marriage vows—a dream assignment I've
waited a lifetime for.*

*And the most wonderful part of this assignment is that I get to write about an amazing product: Robby Scharf.*

*When I first met Robby, I knew I dug him; when he told me he lived for sports, I knew he wasn't a pussy; when I heard he was a Jewish rocker, I knew he was no ordinary Jew; when I found out we were aligned politically, I knew it was a match, and when my father gave him a thumbs-up, I knew he was something special.*

*And when I watched him coach disabled athletes at Special Olympics, I knew I had to have him.*

*But when I fully experienced the depth of his caring and character, I knew it was love.*

*Robby, you are my champion, my protector, my BFF, my favorite comedian, my trusty ad court partner, my own personal IT guy, and my new emergency contact number.*

*You are my Mr. Right in every way.*

*You are the Ashford to my Simpson, Burns to my Allen, the Kool in my Gang, and the Earth and Wind to my Fire. You are music and laughter, safety and comfort, strength and support, every day of my life.*

*I vow to you my love, heart, soul, and spirit. I vow to keep my racquet head up, and keep my eye on the ball. I vow to keep my only-child tendencies in check, and I vow to keep the spare toilet paper in the bathroom instead of in my office closet. I vow to keep an open mind about moving to the Valley, and I vow to learn how to make a brisket and spend more time in the kitchen.*

*As your wife, I vow to keep you happy, healthy, and fit— whether you like it or not. Remember, you're marrying a personal trainer, so deal with it.*

*To your father, Eddie, I vow to make you a good daughter-in-law. Good, in that I will never stand in the way of you and Robby and Major League Baseball.*

*And finally, to your mother, Fran, who is not here with us today, I vow to make her proud. I promise to take good care of her son, and honor the extraordinary man he has become.*

*I've dreamed of writing these vows all my life, and now, this moment is here. Thank you, Robby, for making me your Mrs. Scharf, and for making all my dreams come true.*

Following Jewish tradition, we stomped on the glass and sealed the deal with our first kiss as husband and wife. The crowd went wild. As Robby and I made our way back up the aisle, we high-fived everyone because we knew (as did everyone else) that this was no ordinary wedding. It was a fucking miracle.

By all accounts our wedding was a blowout, and exactly what I dreamed of. People were dancing, drinking, singing, and getting high on the golf course, including my beloved rabbi and makeup artist (both of whom are dear friends from grammar school). And as if it couldn't get any better, I got two fantastic sisters-in-law, Judith and Wendy, and a gem of a father-in-law, Eddie, as early wedding gifts. There was so much love and disbelief in the room, I had to keep pinching myself to see if the whole thing was real.

## A GRADUATE FROM THE DATING SCHOOL OF HARD KNOCKS

Along with fantasy wedding planning, another thing happened in between all my blind dates, bikini waxes, and breakups: I gained wisdom. I had learned so much during my single years that I could've opened my own Dating School of Hard Knocks, with the motto "I fucked up so you don't have to!" carved in stone above its entrance.

My wisdom took a village, and that village included therapists, hypnotherapists, trusted mentors, and intuitive practitioners who taught me about the power of mindfulness, visualization, spiritual healing, and doing deep inner work.

I'm a seeker, so I look for answers anywhere I can find them. If I came across a class or seminar, I'd take it; if I heard about a cool meditation app, I'd download it; if a friend recommended a book, I'd read it; if someone told me to light white candles and stand on my head chanting Sanskrit, I probably would've done it too, because I was on a mission to find my greatness.

Acting as my own client and coach, I knew I had a good chance of succeeding. I had a burning desire to change, was committed to the process, and I was a five-time marathoner who drove a stick shift in LA, so I was no stranger to pain. Most importantly, I had a measure of self-worth that told me I was deserving of better.

To achieve my goals, I became a sponge soaking up every piece of enlightenment I could get my hands on. All of it, I believe, helped me get to the altar.

But even if I hadn't found Robby, even if I had stayed single, it wouldn't have been a waste. I'd still be a happier, healthier person because I took it on. I did exactly what I instruct my clients to do: I dug deep, I faced my fears, and I pushed through the pain like an athlete.

## Succeed Like a Pro

Regardless of their pursuit or project, I know before I even start working with a client whether they're going to succeed or not, based on my following five indicators:

1. **You have a burning desire to change, grow, or improve.** You're fed up with being miserable, overweight, unfulfilled, blocked, or stuck.

2. **You're committed to the process.** You know change takes time, sacrifice, and dedication. Whatever the process requires, however long it takes, you're in it to win it.

3. **You can endure some healthy pain and tough love.** Whether you're exercising to get in shape or exorcising an ex out of your life, there will be pain. People who can tolerate a little discomfort often see faster and longer-lasting results.

4. **You believe it's possible to achieve your goals, and you're capable of making it happen.** It's possible, doable, and within reach.

*continued*

> **5. You have a measure of self-worth.** All the effort in the world means nothing if you don't have a baseline of worthiness. It doesn't matter if it's a great body, a great job, or a great love you want, you must first believe you're deserving of it.

## IT WAS THERE ALL ALONG

Just to be clear, by no means is getting married the end-all, be-all pinnacle of success (anyone who's ever survived divorce can tell you that). You don't need a man to save you, nor do you need marriage or a relationship to complete you. In my case, though, getting married was a defining moment. Since marriage had eluded me for so long, when it finally happened, everything suddenly made sense: My limited beliefs had gotten the best of me.

All my past relationship fails had me believing I was damaged goods. But when I met Robby, I realized I had the goods the whole time. He just showed them to me—or maybe, I was ready to see them myself.

*I know who I am. I know what I've got.* I had it in me all along.

You have the goods and your greatness is in you—but sometimes you need someone to show it to you. As much as I advocate being the source of your own validation, I confess that it's nice to be validated. It's nice having confirmation that you're doing something right, and it's nice to be loved, in whatever form love comes.

For this reason, make sure you surround yourself with people who champion you. Choose friends who root for you. Partner with a mentor or coach who believes in you. Engage in activities that elevate you. And make sure your choices reflect and reinforce your greatness at all times.

Whatever makes you feel proud, boosts your self-esteem, and reminds you on a daily basis that you're pretty fucking awesome is all the validation you'll ever need.

# My Tough-Love Advice to You

If you want to find your greatness, you've got to do the work. You've got to stop making excuses, stop refusing to take responsibility and claiming victimhood. In other words, you're gonna have to start kicking your own ass.

Doing all of this will build your confidence and self-worth. If, however, your self-worth tank is low, here are my go-to tips inspired by Stoic philosophy to fill your tank back up.

1. Own your truth, flaws, and quirks, and use them to your advantage.
2. Practice self-forgiveness and compassion.
3. Take stock of your strengths, talents, accomplishments, and great qualities.
4. Stop all negative internal self-talk.
5. Remember a time when you overcame self-doubt and prevailed.
6. Congratulate yourself for doing the hard things.
7. Be open to compliments and accept them graciously.
8. Celebrate the small wins.
9. Don't compare yourself to others.

The good news is that if you practice the preceding, you'll get results, whether it's succeeding as an empowered single or rocking it as a middle-aged marriage first-timer.

FIFTEEN

# HALF A CENTURY OF BEING SINGLE, BUT WHO'S COUNTING?

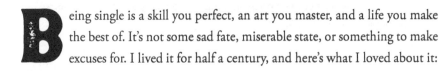

*Be not afraid of growing slowly, be afraid only of standing still.*
—Chinese proverb

**B**eing single is a skill you perfect, an art you master, and a life you make the best of. It's not some sad fate, miserable state, or something to make excuses for. I lived it for half a century, and here's what I loved about it:

- You've got freedom and independence.
- You can make your own decisions, with or without input from others.
- You're the boss of you.
- You can call your own shots and make your own rules.

- You have autonomy and agency.
- You can have all the peace, quiet, and privacy you desire.
- You can keep your home super-clean or like a pigsty.
- You can go out, stay home, have popcorn and beer for dinner, or drink wine in bed.

And if you're not actively dating, you don't have to shave your legs or get waxed on a regular basis. If you're a guy, you can scratch your balls and fart all you want.

Now that's what I call freedom!!

Truth is, there's never been a better time to be single. As satirist Adrian Baylor points out: "Now, women have the ability to live whole, full, happy lives, without ever dating or marrying. Women can have fulfilling orgasms, buy houses, have children, work rewarding jobs, live fulfilling lives, all without ever taking a male partner or needing a man to sign off on her life; it's like suddenly women aren't interested in trading their own bodies and humanity for their basic hierarchy of needs now that women can provide those needs for themselves!"[20]

Nowadays, you can make the first move, ask someone out, even propose to your boyfriend, and no one can say boo about it! Not even me!

## SINGLE LIFE: THE BEST OF TIMES, THE WORST OF TIMES

For some women, single life is the best of times. For others, it's the worst.

Anyone who's ever spent the holidays alone, or a Valentine's Day without a Valentine, knows what I'm talking about. So does anyone who's ever been a singleton at a couples' dinner party, a wedding guest without a plus one, or dateless at a family function. Even the strongest of singles can feel the sting.

For years, a friend of mine threw dinner parties attended mostly by married friends and school parents. Even though I was single, she would invite me,

---

20   Adrian Baylor, "Dating Isn't What It Used to Be for Men. Because of Women," Medium.com, accessed November 16, 2021.

and I accepted because I adore her and she's an incredible cook. The evenings were filled with great food, wine, and fabulously accomplished, mostly partnered people.

Sometimes the dinners were tough to get through because I was neither married, a parent, fabulously accomplished, nor a couple. I was single and struggling to hold my own as I tried to fit in. This was not helped by the fact that I was a fitness trainer, and looked it.

My singleness at times made me feel like an outsider, a party crasher, an alien from another planet, and the last kid picked for a team. I wasn't a member of the married club or the mommy club. There were times I felt ignored, and times I felt stink-eye beamed at me, but I know that was just my paranoid imagination playing tricks on me. No matter how inclusive and hospitable my friend the hostess was, or how lovely her dinner guests were, my insecurities would always get the better of me.

In my paranoid mind the wives hated me, and the husbands didn't talk to me because if they did, the wives would kill them. There's a special stink-eye reserved for husbands who dare chat with you. In times like these, I was aware that my outer appearance was both a blessing and a curse: a blessing that brought me male attention, a curse when women judged me for it.

I wasn't paranoid, though, when a fitness client would remind me how old I was, and how men weren't interested in women my age. This was when I was in my early 40s, and her words of advice were to "find an old guy in his 70s, because that's really all you got." This "advice" would often leave me in tears.

I also wasn't paranoid when a married female acquaintance in my social circle would forget my name every time I saw her. She knew me, knew who I was, where I came from, and who my friends were, and yet at every party she'd say, "I'm sorry, what's your name again?" A subtle dig that confirmed I wasn't welcomed in their coupled-up world.

**When you're single, people secretly suspect you're maybe either too complicated, damaged goods, or a loser.**

When you're single, people judge, stare, question, whisper, gossip, and shame. They make assumptions, view you with suspicion, and jump to conclusions. They ask why you're not married or don't have kids, and they secretly suspect you're maybe either too complicated, damaged goods, or a loser.

## THE PREJUDICE OF SINGLISM

Being single or childless is neither a hardship or tragedy, nor is it a problem to be fixed. Still, the stigma exists. There's even a word for it: "singlism." Coined by social scientist Bella DePaulo, singlism is the technical term for holding negative beliefs about single people, or treating them unfairly because of their single status.[21]

The good news is that if you stay single long enough, the questions will cease. When my mother stopped asking when I was getting married and started asking if I had received my AARP card yet, I knew things were getting better.

But some people aren't so lucky. The questions keep coming. Like the time many years ago when I was in between relationships and I went for a wax. My Russian waxer Esther took one look at the overgrowth, and said in her very thick accent: "Vaht, Treva? No boyfriend?"

The questions never stop. Just ask Jennifer Aniston, the subject of relentless rumors about her marriage and maternal status—stuff of no one's business. In an interview a while ago, she finally told everybody to stop speculating about her happiness. I will tell you the same: You don't need to be married and have kids to be happy, so STFU already!

Shamers and haters come in all shapes and sizes. Sometimes they're fellow single women who view you as a threat or competition. Sometimes they're married women who secretly begrudge your freedom. Sometimes they're former friends with whom you've fallen out and use the falling out as an opportunity to dump their bitterness, resentment, and petty jealousy all over you. Or sometimes they're good friends you thought you could trust, only to have them betray you. I've had some bad romantic breakups in my day, but friend breakups are next-level heartbreak.

As I mentioned in chapter 2, it's important to understand what your part is when there's a problem or conflict. When I have drama with someone, I take a

---

21    Several articles by DePaulo on the topic can be found on her website at
      http://www.belladepaulo.com/category/singlism/.

hard look at what my part is, and then take action to correct it. I've found that when you come from drama it's easy to recreate drama, so I try to be mindful of it.

Admittedly, there were times when I had a hand in the drama; other times, I was a victim of someone's drama. I'm being nice when I say "drama" here. What I'd really like to say is off-the-rails, unhinged, batshit crazy.

This was never more the case than when a friend fallout became so hostile that it devolved into bullying. This ex-friend left nasty comments on my blogs, belittled me on social media, spread vicious gossip, and sent hateful texts. It got so bad, I had a lawyer issue a cease and desist letter to make her stop.

I tell you all this not to dump my own resentment and bitterness, but to illustrate the power of the forgiveness work I talked about in chapter 2. Without forgiveness work, I'd still be holding anger in my heart. With the work, the pain of these memories has lost its power, and my heart finds grace for those who have hurt me.

Part of forgiveness work is staying open to reconciliation and redemption, and the possibility of greater things. Even after being betrayed and bullied, I will always seek to find a new understanding. There's nothing better than making peace and patching things up with a friend, and having your friendship become even stronger because of it.

I also always want to believe the good in people, but the unfortunate truth is that haters, shamers, and mean girls can be an ugly part of singlehood. Female rivalry in general can be ugly—but so can our own self-inflicted hate and shame of being single. Don't add to the narrative. Don't feed into it.

## Assume the Position

Being single can make you feel incredibly insecure and self-conscious. The challenge is to be bigger than it, bigger than the people who judge you. To do this, stand taller than you think you can; hold your head high, pull your shoulders back, and engage your core. Posture is *everything*. You'll not only appear more confident, but you'll also look 10 pounds lighter and 10 years younger. When you have a strong physical presence, you're more able to repel the slings and arrows of stink-eye.

## Make Friends with Your Single Status ASAP

The strongest statement you can make as a single person is to live life on your own terms, without apology. If you make friends with your singleness, chances are that people will make friends with it too. You set the tone for how you want to be seen and treated—so no self-pity, no "woe is me." This is the time to be your biggest fan and cheerleader.

When a person asks: "Why aren't you married yet?" smile and answer, "I'm exercising my options," or "What's wrong with being single?" You don't owe anyone any explanations or excuses. Be charming and gracious, and if they shame you because you're single, shame on them.

## Have a Great Friend of the Opposite Sex

Having a platonic pal to hang out with when you're single is crucial. With opposite sex friends there's no competition, jealousy, or weirdness, just unconditional love, support, and someone to root for you. Guyfriends and girlfriends make great confidantes, escorts, plus ones, and trusty wingmen. Always have one handy and on speed dial.

## Be a Third Wheel and Like It

I owe my married friends a debt of gratitude and a thousand reciprocal dinners for bringing me along with them when I was single. As embarrassed as I was being the third wheel, the truth is, those dinners were important. My married friends got me out, accepted me, fed me, and gave my social life balance. Sometimes it's a nice change of pace to be around couples. If you get an invitation to be a third wheel, go, and make sure you reciprocate by taking them to dinner too.

## Embrace Your Humanness

By the time you hit midlife, you'll have some baggage. Maybe it's a divorce, health or financial issues, an ex, or scar tissue from previous breakups. These aren't marks against you; they're what makes you human. Even your generational trauma makes you human and more relatable.

Your baggage is only as heavy as your underlying thoughts are about it. Your past (and everything that comes with it) gives you depth and character. It's what people resonate with, so turn it into an asset, not a liability. Your humanness isn't a deal-breaker, but it is if you allow it to be.

## Get Good at Rejection

Not everyone is going to like you, and you're not going to like everyone, but that's dating (and life), so get used to it. Rejection hurts, but your ego shouldn't be so inflated or fragile that you can't survive it.

As an athlete, I see everything through the lens of sports—including dating, because to me dating *is* a sport. It's performance, ability, agility, strategy, skills, wins, and losses, and of course, stamina and endurance. If dating is a team try-out, then rejection is getting cut from the team.

**You never want to be with someone who doesn't want to be with you.**

Rejections are hard on the ego, especially if you hate losing, like me. They get into your head, mess with your game, and make you feel like a pro athlete on a losing streak.

That's what happened to me. I wasn't dating relaxed. I wasn't in the zone. I was overthinking everything. When I'd get up to bat, I'd choke. I was so afraid of striking out that I'd strike out. I literally developed performance anxiety from dating.

When you overthink, you can't relax; when you doubt your ability, you can't perform. If you're afraid of failing, you're not flowing. And if your need to put the ball away, end the point, or win the game (or the guy) is too intense, it'll only keep victory away from you.

Another problem with rejections is that they have a sneaky way of feeding into our confirmation bias that somehow, we're undesirable or unworthy of love. This couldn't be further from the truth. No one is out of your league. No one is *ever* too good for you. It's been said a million different ways, but your value doesn't decrease just because someone fails to see it. If someone doesn't want to date you, it doesn't mean you're undatable. If someone doesn't want you, it doesn't mean you're unwantable. You never want to be with someone who doesn't want to be with you.

In case you forget, repeat to yourself: *I know who I am, and I know what I've got.*

The best thing you can do with rejection is use it as an opportunity for growth. Rejection is like muscle, and muscle grows from micro-tears to the tissue when you exercise. With each tear, newer, bigger, stronger muscle is created. It's the same with breakups. You get a little stronger after each one. So don't let rejection get the best of you; make the best of rejection, and let it change you for the better.

After every breakup, I got better. Getting dumped would initially send me into a death spiral, but after regaining my footing I would emerge with a stronger sense of my potential. Part of that was finding my own closure, and not relying on an ex to make me feel better. I took my pain and turned it into a plan to move on as fast as I could.

## Stop Waiting for People to Love You

We do all kinds of things to be loved. We compromise ourselves and abandon our identity; we jump through hoops; we work too hard, wait too long, and people-please the hell out of ourselves. I know because I did this when I was single, and completely lost myself at times.

I wanted to be in a relationship. I wanted to be married. I wanted to be loved. That it was taking so long had me convinced that I wasn't enough, and confirmed that love was out of reach. It didn't stop me from trying, though. I thought if I worked hard enough and waited long enough, someone would eventually see that I was worth marrying.

I eventually found someone, and that someone found me, and love happened because we both were real with each other. No one had to wait or jump through hoops or work too hard. We accepted and loved each other exactly as we were. This didn't happen by magic. It was intentional work on my part to love and accept myself first.

When you wait for someone to love you, you end up handing over your dignity to the person whose love, approval and acceptance you so desperately seek.

We do it in friendship too. We bend over backward and cross our own boundaries for people to like us. It's exhausting, not to mention very demoralizing.

Out of curiosity I did a Google search on "how to make someone love you," and much to my dismay, I found over 1,480,000,000 search results. Apparently, there's a whole industry devoted to being loved, with millions of tricks, mind games, and spells, for all I know.

Here's a few listings I came upon:

- 6 Scientifically Proven Ways to Make Someone Fall for You
- How to Use Psychology to Make Someone Fall (and Stay) in Love with You
- 19 Ways to Help You "Make" Someone Love You
- 12 Ways to Make a Woman Fall Deeply in Love with You
- 15 Tricky Psychological Ways to Make Someone Love You
- 6 Sneaky Ways to Get Him to Say I Love You
- 15 Science-Backed Tips to Make Someone Love You

Reading all this broke my heart because not one of them suggested that the way to get someone to love you is to simply be yourself.

Waiting for people to love you is a complete waste of your precious energy and time, not to mention a complete diss to your self-respect. Dating or wanting to be friends with someone who doesn't feel the same way isn't just a constant reminder of what you can't have, it confirms all your worst fears that you're not enough.

If you keep trying to be what you think someone wants, you will become unrecognizable to yourself, which to me, is more painful than not being loved in the first place.

So don't hold back your truth or stifle the real you. Don't try so hard to win people over, and don't be so fearful that you forget who you are. Believe in yourself, and that alone will win people over.

At the same time, dump the people-pleaser and let the approval-seeker go.

It shouldn't take long for someone to see your magnificence, but if it does, you're with the wrong someone. Move on, don't wait. As dating advice writer

Shani Silver reminds us: "Anyone you have to convince to want you is a prime candidate for deletion."[22]

## IF YOU *DO* GET WHAT YOU WANT

Note to late bloomers: I've found that a weird thing happens when you finally get the thing you've been wanting or waiting for—you freak out. You panic that it's not real, won't last, or that you'll screw it all up. It's called "adjustment shock," and when Robby proposed, I got a dose of it.

Right after I was hit with adjustment shock, I was hit with "imposter syndrome," another side effect of sudden status change. Imposter syndrome is defined as a "psychological pattern in which people doubt their accomplishments and have a persistent, often internalized fear of being exposed as a fraud."[23] My imposter syndrome made me feel like I was a big fake who didn't deserve the proposal to begin with. Because I only saw myself as single, to be anything else was a mistake.

Please, please, please remember that whatever you accomplish later in life, *you earned and deserve.* You waited and worked for it, and there's no mistake about it. Big achievements aren't flukes, and neither are you.

## BE OK WITH BEING SINGLE FOREVER, BECAUSE YOU MIGHT BE

This is going to be a tough pill to swallow, but finding The One or Happily Ever After might take a while—or not at all—so you better get on with it. Start making the best of single life now. Don't watch the clock, don't keep score, and don't compare or compete with others. The only thing you need to do is keep your eyes on the prize—the prize being you.

---

22 Shani Silver, "There's Nothing Wrong with Taking Dating Seriously," October 22, 2020, https://shanisilver.medium.com/there-is-nothing-wrong-with-taking-dating-seriously-1df7216efe26.

23 See Megan Dalla-Camina, "The Reality of Imposter Syndrome," *Psychology Today*, September 3, 2018, https://www.psychologytoday.com/us/blog/real-women/201809/the-reality-imposter-syndrome.

We all know life isn't always fair, and we don't always get what we want. I know this all too well after suffering through so many DNFs. Yet to spend one more minute lingering in what didn't finish would detract from what I could finish. Even without a partner, I'd go on and be happy. What were my choices? Live a miserable single life? Hell no.

I don't care how lonely you get or how badly you want a partner—twisting yourself into knots to be in a relationship, or being in a relationship and wishing you were single, is the very definition of misery. So is endlessly scrolling and swiping on dating apps to no avail.

I have news for you: You don't have to date if you don't want to.

You can call off your search for The One right now and be free! Delete your apps, burn your bra, and be a liberated single babe! Don't wait to be Happily Ever After; build a life you love, this minute, on your own, design it how you want, and be happily ever after right now!

Before you get too excited though, there's something I need to warn you about. When you make peace without The One, you just might meet The One. Sorry to break it to you.

Speaking of making peace, to the bullies of the world, I have a favor to ask: Please soften your hearts and don't be mean. Women need each other more than ever, so be allies, not enemies.

There are some things I don't miss about being single, like suffering through a married couple dinner party by myself. Having a partner in tow definitely helps ward off stink-eye if you're the only singleton at a soiree, but you shouldn't need one to hold your own. The only shield you need to ward off stink-eye is your own sense of self.

Other things I miss about being single? Not shaving my legs and letting my pubes grow out. That's a thing of the past now, and no one's happier about it than Robby and my waxer Esther, who are both down there on a regular basis.

# SURVIVAL OF THE FITTEST: CONQUERING LOVE OF ALL KINDS

*If you're going through hell, keep going.*
—Winston Churchill

**L**ooking back on my single years, it's amazing I didn't lose all hope, go into a major depression, or end up in the loony bin. Actually, I did get depressed and lose all hope, but I managed to stay out of the loony bin.

Whether you're entering singlehood for the first time or have been single forever, it can be a tough MF'er. But so can being in a relationship. Or being married. Love is a beautiful calling, whether it's the love you cultivate for a partner or the love you nurture for yourself. Both require work and dedication.

I saw relationships and marriages all around me, with my friends and family having some of the best. As I marveled at their commitment, I also couldn't help wondering how they did it.

And then I got married and saw for myself.

What a noble challenge! What a worthy endeavor! What an amazing pact and promise to make to your beloved and yourself. I've learned that it's sacred and precious, and to be handled with great care.

It takes work to be happy and healthy, and many of the skills I used to keep me happy and healthy when I was single, I use to keep me happy and healthy as a married person. I still have boundaries, I still meet my own emotional needs first, and I always know my value.

**There's no such thing as happily married couples, only happy people that make couples.**

I once read that there's no such thing as happily married couples, only happy people that make couples. The same things that make you a happy single make you a happy spouse. You're always going to be you, regardless of your relationship status.

There's a funny old joke that men marry women hoping they'll never change, and women marry men hoping they will. I'm going with the guys on this. The person you fell in love with when you met should remain as close to being that same person after you marry. And if they do change, it should be for the right reasons. Marriage hasn't changed me. I'm still the same person, just ever-evolving.

To help you survive, thrive, and conquer love of any kind, here are my favorite tips.

## KNOW YOUR VALUE

Knowing your value is knowing you deserve more, deserve better, and refuse to settle until you get both. When you know your worth you'll never grovel, be a victim, or sell out. You'll recover quicker from rejection, heal faster from breakups and shrug off disappointment easier.

After you've determined your value, determine the value of the people you date. Are they worthy of *you*? Are they deserving of *your* love? Have they earned the honor and privilege of being with *you*?

When you know this, you increase your value to *yourself*.

## RAISE YOUR BAR

When you raise your bar for what's acceptable and non-negotiable, you automatically feel better about yourself. You'll see the quality of your dating life improve, you'll become more discerning, and whatever you lose in certain relationships, you'll gain in sanity and self-respect.

## STAY ON THE PATH OF RIGHT ACTION

Staying on the path of right action means making good choices, using good judgment, and not putting yourself in harm's way. Simply put, it means not doing stupid shit. Anyone who's gotten involved with a crazy chick, a boss, a bad boy, or a hot mess knows what I'm talking about. I like to call people like this *tsuris magnets* ("tsuris" is Yiddish for trouble), because they attract trouble.

Many singletons make mistakes in the name of wanting a relationship. They confuse sex for love, but love isn't sex, and sex isn't love. Also, sex isn't power, and drama isn't passion.

Before you do something potentially unwise, ask yourself: What purpose will it serve, and will it benefit my life, career, or get me closer to my goals? If the answer is no, then you must fight the urge to be stupid with every self-respecting bone in your body.

One of the greatest pieces of advice I've ever heard came from a client whose mother used to tell her "Don't go looking for something that may hurt you."

This is where "upper limit problems" come in. Coined by bestselling author and personal growth pioneer Gay Hendricks, upper limit problems (ULPs) are obstacles we put up to keep us from succeeding and keep us repeating old patterns and habits. ULPs keep us stuck in our comfort zone, even if that comfort is fear and loathing. It's the ultimate self-sabotage.[24]

To make sure you're not self-sabotaging, try to see yourself in the third person and observe your behavior and actions. See if they match the vision of the person

---

24   Gay Hendricks, *The Big Leap: Conquer Your Hidden Fear and Take Life to the Next Level* (New York: HarperOne, 2010).

you want to be. If real love is what you want, if a stable relationship is what you crave, if security and companionship are what you seek, then stay on the path of right action.

## TAKE A LOOK AT YOUR OWN RED FLAGS

We point fingers all day long at people who let us down; we're quick to place blame without taking responsibility; we look out for warning signs in others, but fail to see them in ourselves. Maybe it's time to look at your own red flags. You're the common denominator in all your relationships, so the examination must start with you. Ask yourself:

- Am I being too reactive?
- Can I do more to improve my life and emotional health?
- Can I listen more, talk less?
- Am I pushing people away out of fear?
- Do I have old traumas that keep getting triggered?
- Am I coming from a place of insecurity?
- Am I seeing myself the way other people see me?

Remember, if you want to change your situation, you first have to change yourself—and looking at your own red flags is a good place to start. It's not only an act of self-love if you're single, it's a loving act for your partner.

## SET YOUR BOUNDARIES

Setting boundaries is self-preservation, full stop. Speaking up, standing up for yourself, drawing the line, and knowing your limits are part of boundary-setting. So is having the courage to say "no."

I had no clue what "boundaries" meant until a therapist once told me I had none. Out of an overwillingness to be a good girlfriend, dutiful daughter, or helpful friend, I took it all on, and often got burned. I was a classic people-pleaser who couldn't say no.

The question is, why are you saying "yes" in the first place? Is it to avoid conflict or to avoid doing your own work? Is it to feel needed, useful, or loved?

My mother had a saying I apply to setting boundaries: "A virtue when misused becomes a vice." To want to help is virtuous, but when it interferes with your life—or takes away from it—it becomes a vice. Saying "yes" isn't always good, and saying "no" isn't always bad—know the difference.

Setting boundaries is hard because you feel guilty you're not doing enough. Saying "no" is hard because you feel like you're letting people down. Doing both, though, will set you free.

As important as boundary-setting is, so is establishing your non-negotiables. Non-negotiables are your absolute must-haves based on what you feel you deserve and can tolerate. Boundaries and non-negotiables go hand in hand because you can't really do one without the other.

Having no boundaries is like springing leaks in a boat. Saying "yes" when you shouldn't, agreeing when you don't want to, or giving of yourself to people who don't appreciate it all spring leaks in your boat. Your boat is your psyche, and those holes leak out your value.

Saying yes = more leaks = a sinking boat.

Plug the holes, throw the people-pleaser overboard, and watch your boat rise.

## DON'T MAKE FINDING A MAN OR WOMAN YOUR SOLE MISSION IN LIFE

Thankfully I had other things going on when I was single, or else I would've sent every last guy running. As much as I wanted to be in a relationship, I was careful not to make it my life's purpose.

I got involved with other pursuits. I became a mentor to at-risk kids, I joined a mixed doubles tennis team, I started a meditation practice, and got politically active. Having these outlets took my mind off dating, and the pressure off any one guy to fulfill my every need (which is impossible). And guess what happened? I met guys while doing it.

The same goes for making your partner or spouse the center of your world, to the exclusion of other things. A singular focus on someone isn't healthy. Marriage hasn't stopped me from my hobbies and pursuits—however, my hobbies and pursuits have brought a lot to my marriage.

Instead of training a laser focus on getting a guy, focus on something equally worthy, like picking up a new skill or hobby, rescuing a pet, volunteering, or joining a Meetup group. Engaging in good-for-your-soul activities not only takes the edge off of dating, it also adds dimension to your relationship if you're coupled up.

Find other things to love and you'll not only find purpose and meaning; you might find love while you're at it.

## LET THE "ONE THAT GOT AWAY" GET AWAY

Everybody has that one person that "got away." The truth is, they didn't really get away, you let them go, and probably for good reason: either the relationship wasn't working, you weren't ready, you didn't feel the love, you couldn't settle down, or didn't want to settle. You did what was right at the time, so don't regret your decision and don't look back. By letting them go, you released yourself to find someone/something better.

## HAVE A RELATIONSHIP WITH YOURSELF

The most important relationship you're ever going to have is with yourself, so it better be a good one.

Too many people jump into relationships because they can't be alone; they can't be at one with their thoughts, or fear they can't make it on their own. They need company to distract them from solitude and stillness. When you fear being alone, you increase your risk of settling for the wrong people.

Even when I was at my most excruciating singleness—in my 40s with a biological clock going berserk—I could still be alone, and my own company was enough.

If you can master solitude, you'll never be needy. If you can learn to be your own best friend, you'll never be lonely.

## MEET YOUR OWN EMOTIONAL NEEDS FIRST

Taking responsibility for your emotional well-being is what mature adults do, single or not.

We'd all love to get assurances, promises, certainty, and approval from others, but life doesn't always work that way. You can't demand it or depend on it. Your boyfriend, girlfriend, or spouse can only make you feel secure, attractive, and loved up to a point—the rest is up to you. You need to meet your own needs first.

The only child in me is here to tell you it's possible; I've had to meet my own emotional needs all my life. But the only child in me is also here to remind you that you're human, and humans need assurance sometimes. For the reasons I laid out in chapter 14, it's good to have people in your life who can validate you when you need it.

Even the securest of us worry—about love, relationships, the future. We go to dark places and fill our minds with self-doubt and irrational fear. We work ourselves into a tizzy, or in my case, a middle-of-the-night sweaty menopausal panic.

When panic hits me I take a few deep breaths to the top of my lungs, hold them, and then exhale fully, allowing the fear to release. After a few minutes, I'm able to get my head back on straight. I've found that moments like this can be avoided (or at least mitigated) by having a love for yourself that's so rock solid that no amount of irrational fear can shake it. Hormone replacement also helps, at least for the night sweats!

If you can meet your own needs first and communicate what you need from others, you'll set up your future relationships for success.

## TEMPER YOUR EXPECTATIONS
## (AND YOUR NEED FOR CONTROL)

Expectations are a form of needing control. When you have expectations you're projecting into the future, and you're not in the present. You're anxious about what's next. With Robby, I consciously threw out my expectations (and need for control) and allowed things to unfold. Because I enjoyed his company so much, I didn't care where it went.

When dating, the best strategy is to go in without an agenda and expect nothing. That way, you'll avoid disappointment if things don't work out, and be pleasantly surprised if they do. This is called "detaching from the outcome."

Detach from the things you can't control and focus on the things you can—like your thoughts, actions, and attitude. You can always hope for the best; you can have aspirations, just not expectations.

## HAVE FRIENDS YOU CAN COUNT ON

Whether you're single or partnered, having a solid network of friends is like the old Playtex bra commercial tagline: "Support can be beautiful." As a perpetual single and only child, my friends became family, and girlfriends became sisters. They were there for me when I was a kid, there for me when I was single, and they're with me now that I'm married and older. I love them for being so righteously steadfast and solid—cherish those.

Relationships may come and go, love may or may not last, friendships may not go the distance, but the good ones do.

This reminds me of a quote I read years ago (from an unknown author): "There comes a point in your life when you realize: who matters, who never did, who won't anymore, and who always will. So don't worry about people from your past, there's a reason why they didn't make it to your future."

## COUNT YOUR BLESSINGS

I know it's cliche, and I've mentioned it many times, but taking stock of what you have, instead of what you don't, gives life fullness when it feels empty.

Just reminding myself that I'm not in a wheelchair from my car accident years ago is enough to shake off whatever petty grievance or temporary sadness I may be experiencing.

Thanks to whoever said, "Happiness isn't about getting what you want all the time. It's about loving what you have and being grateful for it."

I don't care if you're single or married: Find some piece of gratitude, some little thing to be thankful for every day (like supportive family, good friends, loyal clients, a steady job, good health), and you'll feel a shift and a lift.

And don't just quietly be grateful for family, friends, and clients—*tell* them to their face how grateful you are. Acknowledge them and thank them. Tell them how much they mean to you. Expressing your love and appreciation will give them a shift and a lift.

## ADMIT YOU HATE BEING SINGLE

As you know, I'm a big supporter of singlehood. To my single brothers and sisters, you've got my respect.

Going solo is an admirable pursuit, but if you secretly hated it, I'd understand. Singlehood isn't always a picnic, and it's OK to admit it.

It's OK to admit you want companionship. It's OK to admit you're lonely. It's OK to admit you've had enough solitude. It's OK to admit you're not OK.

In recent years there seems to be a militant backlash to couplehood, with singles voicing their righteous indignation through blogs, dating forums, and Reddit threads. I feel like it's another issue in the culture wars, like gay rights or women's rights; we now have singles fighting for their rights not to marry or be in relationships.

The narrative on singlehood needs to change. Single people are mad and I can't blame them. They're mad because society makes them feel like second-class citizens, and mad because couples often get preferential treatment. At the same time, though, the narrative on wanting to love and be loved needs to change too.

In the last chapter I listed some great things about being single—like making meals out of beer and popcorn and drinking wine in bed. I still love those things, and enjoy me-time, but I also love being a partner and I'm not afraid to say it:

- It's nice having a play date every day who spoons me at night.
- It's fun having someone to run errands and do chores with.

- I love having my husband as my emergency contact.
- I love being called "Mrs. Scharf."
- If one of us farts, there's always someone to hear it and laugh.
- It's nice having someone there when I'm scared.
- Home feels less empty with another person in it.

There's nothing wrong with wanting to share your life with someone. You're not a whiner or less woke; you're human.

As humans, we are wired to connect. We are social animals; it's in our DNA, so why deny it? Why shame people for wanting a partner, or worse, shame yourself because you want one too? Being single isn't always a badge of honor; the truth is that sometimes it sucks.

I didn't complain much about being single, but there were times in my mid-30s when I would become painfully aware of it. For some strange reason, it would hit me while I was washing my dishes after dinner. I'd be standing at the kitchen sink, and this weird loneliness would creep over me. Nowhere else would this happen. I'd feel a visceral quiet in my apartment and become acutely aware that I was totally alone. "It's like staring into the empty void," as my friend Meredyth once described moments like this.

To snap myself out of the empty void I'd dry my hands, pick up the phone, and call my father. He'd always assure me that it was normal, and admit he often felt lonely too as a single dad. He told me what I used to tell him: "Everything's going to be all right."

———

Single or not, life, as we know, can be a tough MF'er. There will be times when you get depressed, lose all hope, and think you'll end up in the loony bin, but those are exactly the moments you find out what you're made of and realize that much to your surprise, you're stronger than you think.

So next time you're going through hell, keep going. It's what Winston Churchill and I would want you to do.

# DONE BEING SINGLE, THE PODCAST

*While we teach, we learn.*

—Seneca

In his book *Outliers*, author Malcolm Gladwell popularized the 10,000-hour rule, which claims if you spend 10,000 hours doing something you will reach a level of mastery that qualifies you as an expert. [25] Whether or not this has been proven, I can certainly say I've spent close to 10,000 hours dating—so I like to think I've reached a level of mastery enough to qualify myself as a dating expert.

Robby, on the other hand, isn't comfortable with the "expert" moniker, even though as a 57-year-old marriage first-timer he clocked in a few thousand dating hours in his day. Between the two of us, we joke that we have 107 years of single life under our belts. We're not sure whether that makes us experts or losers.

---

25   Malcolm Gladwell, *Outliers: The Story of Success* (Boston: Little, Brown, 2008).

## A PODCAST IS BORN

Three years into our marriage, VoiceAmerica Talk Radio Network gave us an opportunity to take all our dating mastery (and misery) and turn it into a podcast called *Done Being Single*. It was inspired by my blog *The Late-Blooming Bride*, where as you know, I dispensed advice on dating and finding love later in life.

To get started, Robby set up an incredible studio in his home office and equipped it with high-quality mics and headphones (he had been in the pro audio business for many years and has great gear). Even though we were first-time podcasters with zero on-air experience, our sound quality was excellent. I'm not sure if this was a good thing, since you could probably hear our every flub that much more clearly. VoiceAmerica supplied us with a producer and engineer, and every Saturday at 12 p.m. Pacific Time, we went live.

Turns out, we were naturals. We had the kind of chemistry and confidence that could've passed for well-seasoned talk radio pros. Most of all, we had authenticity, and a delightful lack of polish that I think is part of our charm. We're probably a broadcaster's nightmare, but somehow our little show garnered over 300,000 active listeners all over the world.

Maybe because we're brutally honest with ourselves and our audience, and they appreciate that. We sit next to each other and talk as if we're not on the air. Listening to us is like being a fly on the wall. We dig into our past, tackle tough issues, share our marital woes and complaints about aging, and how we're dealing with elderly parents. Mostly, we psychoanalyze our listeners' dating dys-functions and work them out on the air.

As great as our rapport is, our styles are actually quite different. Robby is a strict producer, and I like to wing it. We never have a script to read from—just a bio of our guest, some probing questions, and a sound board of funny sound effects. In our podcast world nothing is off-limits, and everything is on the table. No one is filtered, either, especially me.

Sometimes winging it doesn't always work. In fact, many times we don't agree and get into fights on-air. We give each other dirty looks, make hand gestures, and may not speak to each other for hours after we wrap. Robby thinks I talk over him, and I think he's too exacting.

We're both right. I can't control my mouth, and he can't control his strict professional standards. When we were audio only, we were able to hide our annoyance because no one could see us (on one episode I was so mad at Robby that I gave him the silent treatment, which I'm sure was audible). When we went to video and started our own YouTube channel, we became nicer because everyone could see us. I still talked over him, we still made hand gestures, and rolled our eyes, but Robby could edit it out.

One part nerdy science, one part comedy hour, one part true confessions, *Done Being Single* is hilarious, unpredictable, and hopefully, always informative. That was by design. Even though we're technically a "dating podcast," I wanted it to be as inclusive and user-friendly as possible. The goal was to create a sense of community for our listeners, regardless of their relationship status.

Even people who weren't done being single got something out of our show. Episodes featuring our single friends like "What Women Really Want" and "Men, What Say You?" were two of our most popular, as were episodes about sex and divorce.

Even though most of our shows are aimed at midlife singles, our content is designed to be for all ages, because it's never too late or too early to learn about love. I often mused that if I'd had a podcast like this when I was younger and single, it probably would've saved me a lot of time and heartache.

Many episodes are dedicated to marriage—which was useful for me and Robby when we started, since we were still sort of newlyweds figuring out how to be married. We also had to figure out how to cohost a podcast with your spouse. The joke was that our podcast was like getting free couples therapy, which we probably needed after doing the podcast in the first place.

Thankfully, our episode with author and relationship counselor John Gray came to the rescue. John wrote the bestseller *Men Are from Mars, Women Are from Venus,* and that's exactly what Robby and I were finding out. We're from different planets.

Our podcast shows us our problem areas. We've got different communication styles, which isn't necessarily a bad thing if we both would just shut up and listen. Kidding, not kidding. Sometimes you don't want words, you just want to be heard.

I brought this up to John on the show, and he set us straight. It all comes down to feminine and masculine energy.

Feminine energy sometimes just needs to feel connection, and the last thing it needs is masculine energy that wants to fix it or change you at that moment. The irony is, what you're really looking for is a different kind of masculine energy. Masculine energy solves problems, and the problem you're having is you're not feeling connected. So if a man has an understanding of women, he'll pull out his superpower problem solver and recognize words aren't what she needs, action is what she needs. And the action she needs is silence and affection.[26]

He was nailing it, so Robby and I shut up and continued to let him speak:

"Women want a man to listen, and the man will go, 'I am listening,' but then he jumps in with his solutions, when he really needs to jump in with understanding and empathy."

Podcast and marriage saved! If not for John's sage advice, we would've had to rename our show *Done Being Married*.

## WHEN THE STUDENT IS READY, THE TEACHER WILL APPEAR

Robby and I came to the podcast with little experience in long-term commitment—and admitted it. Far from know-it-alls in the area of relationships, we recruited true experts in the field to supplement our education.

Since the show started, we've interviewed world-renowned therapists, relationship experts, social scientists, neuroscientists, sex educators, doctors, business leaders, personal growth influencers, bestselling authors, TED Talk speakers, and thought leaders of all kinds. It's like a jam session of brilliance every time we record a show. The vibe is loose, the topic substantive, and the discussion always hard-hitting.

Our topics range from dating tips to divorce, addiction to attachment theory,

---

26    John Gray, "Are Men Still from Mars and Women from Venus?," *Done Being Single* with Treva and Robby Scharf, July 25, 2019, https://donebeingsingle.com/are-men-still-from-mars-women-from-venus/.

sex tips to social media, politics to performance anxiety, manscaping to money, dating intervention to dating in a pandemic. We examine just about every aspect of love—how to find it, keep it, and not ruin it.

A few episodes stand out for me not just for the sheer amount of info and inspiration they provided, but because our guests confirmed what I've always felt about dating.

For example, people who claim they are too picky really *aren't* picky— they're really just insecure, and use "I'm just picky" as an excuse to hide it. On the other hand, I've found that younger singles use the "I'm too picky" excuse not because they're insecure, but because they're overly secure, and have an inflated sense of their own specialness. In our episode "Too Picky or Not Picky Enough," intimacy expert Allana Pratt backed me up with this:

> One of the things to look at if you're too picky, it's often an excuse to not get vulnerable and to let them see your wobbly parts. If you're not picky enough, you haven't done the inner work to soothe little you who doesn't feel good enough for love, deserving of love, and so you go for anybody, "Do you have a pulse? Do you have a checkbook? Let's do it. Let's get married." You're not balanced on the inside, so it's always important to do the next level of intimacy with self and body, and the divine on the inside. Let's have that communion on the inside, and then oh my god, it becomes so easy. "Here I am, the good, the bad, the ugly. Nice to meet you."[27]

To that I'd add that when you feel undeserving of love, not only do you go for anybody, you also go for nobody.

On the heels of Allana's episode came our episode "Is 'Good Enough' Good Enough?," with author and psychotherapist Lori Gottlieb. We discussed the

---

27    Allana Pratt, "Nobody's Perfect: Are You Too Picky or Not Picky Enough?," *Done Being Single* with Treva and Robby Scharf, March 10, 2018, https://donebeingsingle.com/nobodys-perfect-are-you-too-picky-or-not-picky-enough/.

term "settling," because to Lori, settling doesn't mean compromising on what makes people happy in relationships. It means being intentional in seeking out the qualities that actually lead to loving, lasting marriages:

> It's not about picking someone you're not attracted to or interested in, it's about having higher standards, not lower standards about the things that matter. So often people settle even though they think they're not. They pick people that don't treat them well, or aren't into them, and they are obsessed with that person. That to me is settling.[28]

To Robby, the "Is 'Good Enough' Good Enough?" episode was one of the best, because it put a much-needed new spin on settling. It also inspired Robby to give a much-needed piece of dating advice to our midlife audience:

> Settling isn't a bad word if it's understood that nobody gets 100% of what they want in a mate. We all have to settle at some point and decide if the person we're with is actually who we want to be with. Once you make this decision, it's imperative that you embrace your mate 100%, which will enable you both to soar to greater heights in your relationship. The various insecurities you both felt before will go away. Of course, if you're with someone and your unhappiness ratio is greater than your happiness ratio then "settling" wouldn't be a good thing and making a move or getting out would be the better choice.

We may not have earned expert status by doing the podcast, but we're definitely closer to that distinction. At the very least, we've become enlightened

---

28    Lori Gottlieb, "Is 'Good Enough' Good Enough?," *Done Being Single* with Treva and Robby Scharf, April 14, 2018, https://donebeingsingle.com/is-good-enough-good-enough/.

scholars, thanks to our guests. They continue to teach us so much about love, life, and the human condition.

—

*Done Being Single* showed us that there's so much more to dating than just dating, and so much more to single life than just being single. There's mental health, wellness, self-care, ethics, finance, business, and personal development. There's an owner's manual to being a successful single and to being in a successful partnership.

After all the shows we recorded, interviews, and listener feedback, my biggest takeaway from hosting the *Done Being Single* podcast has been this: Dating is really just an exercise in self-worth.

## BEING "BACKABLE"

Our guests had many ways to define and build self-worth, but one guest in particular hit it out of the ballpark: Suneel Gupta.

Gupta is an entrepreneur and author of the book *Backable: The Surprising Truth Behind What Makes People Take a Chance on You.*[29] He has nothing to do with dating, but his business acumen makes great dating advice, so we invited him on the show.

In dating, that "certain something," that intangible special quality, is often called the "it factor." In business, that same certain something is known as being "backable."

Being backable in the corporate world has nothing to do with looks, charm, swagger, or charisma. Rather, it has everything to do with *conviction*. Gupta says that the best way to sell yourself is to believe in yourself, and I think the same thing applies to dating.

---

29   Suneel Gupta, *Backable: The Surprising Truth Behind What Makes People Take a Chance on You* (Boston: Little, Brown, 2021).

As Gupta explained on our podcast, "Backable people take the time to convince themselves first, then they simply let that conviction shine through whatever style feels most natural. If you want to convince others, you must convince yourself first."[30]

To me, the essence of self-worth is *having conviction about who you are.* This theme ran through every show, regardless of topic or guest. Wherever the conversation went, it always circled back to self-worth.

## COACHING FROM THE INSIDE OUT

A funny thing happened as we were doing *Done Being Single.* All those hours talking about personal growth got me thinking about my own personal growth. The podcast that started off as a hobby became a career-changer for me.

As a fitness trainer, I had achieved a level of mastery with my practice. I had success stories with all of my clients, but I wanted to go deeper. They say trainers are like therapists, which is true; not because my clients told me their problems, but because I could get them faster results *because* of their problems.

I knew what made them tick. I knew the source of their discontent, and I could read them. I knew why they couldn't lose the weight, or stay disciplined, or why they stayed stuck in a body they didn't like.

To me, fitness is an inside job, and I got my clients fit from the inside out.

Because I have an intuitive ability to identify problems and challenges, I decided to take my ability to the next level and become a life coach. I got my credentials from the International Coaching Federation and never looked back.

Goodbye gym, hello fitness of another kind!

While booking talent for our podcast, I discovered there are literally thousands of dating coaches with secret sauces for attracting men and women. The coaches we have on our show are top-notch and well-respected in the dating community, but few if any have what I have: a background as a lifelong athlete

30    Suneel Gupta, "The 'It Factor' and How to Get It," *Done Being Single* with Treva and Robby Scharf, February 19, 2021, https://donebeingsingle.com/the-it-factor-and-how-to-get-it/.

and a lifetime of singlehood. So I combined those areas and found my niche. I took what worked for me as a trainer and translated it into dating coaching.

As a coach, I can make you more irresistible, teach you how to flirt, or give you tricks to snag a man. But that's not my aim. My coaching mission isn't so much about "getting a guy" as it is about getting a life.

My goal as a coach is to improve your emotional fitness, which in turn makes you more irresistible. If I'm going to teach you how to use your feminine wiles or manly charm for anything, it's to be authentic. That's my secret sauce.

Having done more than 10,000 hours of dating, and recording over 120 episodes of *Done Being Single*, I've learned that the most appealing thing a person can have is the conviction to be themselves.

EIGHTEEN

# CONFESSIONS OF OTHER LATE-BLOOMING BRIDES

*Time and patience are the strongest warriors.*

—Leo Tolstoy

A s I mentioned in the introduction, I'm not the only late-blooming bride with a story to tell. There are many of us out there, but two in particular came to mind when I started writing this book: Arielle Ford and Karin Anderson Abrell.

Their stories are very similar to mine. In their 20s and 30s they worked, built their careers, and dated and dated, then finally, as they entered their 40s, they met their person and got married.

I wanted to include Arielle and Karin in my book because they inspire hope: not just for singles or midlifers, but for everyone who's endeavored to find love. Arielle and Karin are wise women. They understand the struggle; they've walked the walk, and their insights provide powerful testimony. As older marriage first-timers they exemplify the benefits of waiting, and are staunch supporters of not settling or selling out.

I want their reflections on singlehood to reassure late bloomers that they're in good company—because it really doesn't matter how old you are, love happens when it happens, which Arielle and Karin know all too well.

If you haven't heard of Arielle Ford, let me introduce you. Arielle is a leading force in the personal growth and contemporary spirituality movement. For the past 30 years she has been living, teaching, and promoting consciousness through all forms of media. She is a celebrated love and relationship expert, author, speaker, and is the cocreator and host of Evolving Wisdom's *Art of Love* series. Her mission is to help women "find love, keep love, and be love."

Arielle's a gifted writer and author of 11 books, including the international bestseller *The Soulmate Secret: Manifest the Love of Your Life with the Law of Attraction* (published in 21 languages and 40 countries).[31] She's also a fellow midlife marriage first-timer who tied the knot at 44 to her beloved Brian.

My friend and Instagram "Dating Hot Takes" partner Dr. Karin Anderson Abrell, PhD, is a psychology professor, therapist, podcast host, author, and advocate for empowered single women. She is a powerhouse of brains and beauty. Her book *Single Is the New Black: Don't Wear White 'Til It's Right*, teaches women how to "stay true to themselves and never settle for anything less than an extraordinary relationship."[13] And that's exactly what she did when she finally met her husband, Dan.

My conversations with Arielle and Karin include their "confessions" on learning from their mistakes, having regrets, keeping the faith, staying strong, and finding love. Their answers were profound and very poignant, and I related to everything they said.

---

31    Arielle Ford, *The Soulmate Secret: Manifest the Love of Your Life with the Law of Attraction* (New York: HarperOne, 2008).

32    Karin Anderson Abrell, *Single Is the New Black: Don't Wear White 'Til It's Right* (Cincinnati: Clifton Hills Press, 2015).

I spoke to Arielle and Karin separately by phone and asked them the same questions about their road to "I do." Not unsurprisingly, it was long and winding—just like mine.

## MY INTERVIEW WITH ARIELLE FORD

**Treva: I hate this question when I'm asked because there is no one answer, but why do you think you were single for so long?**

**Arielle:** Well, I really sucked at relationships. That's sort of the big picture. I was a first-time bride at 44, because I was constantly choosing from a very uninformed place. I had this real desire to be with Captain of the Universe types, the really super successful, ultra-confident guys who were very focused on their career, which of course left them no time to be focused on me, which is what my soul was most calling for. Until I figured that piece out, I was dating and having relationships, but I was always in a state of massive disappointment and dissatisfaction.

When I was 43, I woke up one morning and realized that I did want to find a soulmate and a lifelong partner. So I did sort of an autopsy of my relationship life, and that's where I came to the conclusion that the problem was really me. I was choosing to hang out with the wrong kind of men.

I did a really deep dive into what my soul was most calling for. What kind of man did I need for a lifelong partner?

First and foremost, I wanted a man who was really generous, not generous so much with his money. I was making enough money. I wanted a man who was generous with his time, his love, his affection, and his appreciation. Somebody to actually build a life with. From there, I started using all of the manifestation techniques I had learned over the previous 10 years, and put them all to work to manifest a soulmate.

**Treva: You seem so accomplished from an early age. Did you identify as a late bloomer?**

**Arielle:** I've been a late bloomer my whole life in everything that I've done, and I think it's good. I don't know that I was mature enough a minute sooner than

I was to appreciate the kind of man that Brian is, because I was always gauging by other standards and looking for other things. And I didn't even know what to look for. So had we met when I was 22 or 32, it would have never worked, for him or for me. Neither one of us was ready.

**Treva: When you were growing up, what kinds of messages did you get about marriage?**

**Arielle:** Not good ones. My parents literally hated each other. And so for me, marriage equaled war. It was a constant battle. It was two miserable people making each other more miserable. So I didn't get any good marriage information there.

**Treva: What kind of messages did you get about men?**

**Arielle:** I got one very solid message from my mother: that all men are idiots. I worked through that one in therapy, though, and it's true some men are idiots, just as some women are idiots, but not all men are idiots. I had to lose that one.

**Treva: Did you have moments where you wanted to give up on finding a partner?**

**Arielle:** I think there were a few moments here and there, but I never, for some crazy reason, never doubted that I would find somebody someday. I thought that of course he was very late, and I was late, but I didn't doubt that it would happen eventually.

**Treva: I'm a big believer in attachment theory. What attachment style do you see yourself as—secure, anxious, or avoidant? And which do you want in a partner?**

**Arielle:** I wouldn't say that I was attracted to avoidant types necessarily. They were just busy types, you know. They were super hyperambitious. Because I thought I was super hyperambitious, and I thought it'd be good to be part of a power couple where you have two super hyperambitious people together. I've rarely seen that work, because what I understand now is that there can only be one rock star per family. You need somebody who can be the nurturer and the giver.

**Treva: We're both child-free, but unlike me, you didn't spend years trying to conceive. Can you tell me about that part of your journey?**

**Arielle:** I was never interested in having children and didn't want to ever be anybody's mother. Back in the days when I was doing PR, Kenny Loggins was one of my clients. He's a rock star, and was really big at the time.

We were talking one day, and I told him I never wanted to have kids, he just freaked out because he has five kids. He said, "Oh, no!" He goes, "Someday you're going to turn 50 and you're going to be so depressed that you never had kids. Kids are the greatest things in the world. You really need to go to therapy." He said, "And I'm going to buy you your first session with my therapist."

So I ended up spending a year in therapy specifically on the issue of having kids, and at the end of the year, the therapist said to me, "You know what? You really don't want to have kids, and you don't really need to have kids, and you shouldn't have kids"—after I spent God knows how much money. She just confirmed what I already knew.

On the first day that I met Brian, before—I mean, I really didn't know him at all—I told him on that first date, I will never have children, and you just need to know that up front. And he just looked at me and said, "I'm totally OK with that."

**Treva: Did you make mistakes or have any regrets on your journey to find love?**

**Arielle:** Oh, yeah, I made mistakes every single day. I remember I was in a two-year relationship with this guy and I didn't realize how controlling I was. I actually drew up a contract I wanted him to sign, that basically guaranteed he would call me twice a day, and that we would do certain things on certain days. He was a lawyer, and when he saw the contract, we went to therapy.

**Treva: Singleness can have the side effect of becoming too controlling—of yourself and others. For me, control was a self-preservation mechanism, meant to spare me pain. Did you find the same?**

**Arielle:** I thought I was so right, and he thought I was just really losing it. And the therapist was the one who really pointed out that this was not the way to have a healthy relationship, and I was just being controlling. And the fact that he wouldn't do what I wanted him to do didn't mean that he didn't love me, but because I was in this anxious mode, I just thought I would be happier if he would do things my way.

So I actually broke up with him, although I was very sad about the whole thing. I realized we just weren't a match. We didn't want the same things. We broke up, and he ended up getting married and having a kid within a year of that.

I realized we just weren't meant to be together. And then of course once I met Brian, it was like, oh, thank God this didn't work out, because I could have never been happy with him. We didn't want the same things.

**Treva: At a certain point, if someone hasn't met the right person and sees the reality of being single forever, they may need to have a difficult conversation with themselves. Have you seen this in your coaching work?**

**Arielle:** I come across a lot of women I coach that have that conversation every day, but they don't really mean it. They have this desire for connection and companionship, but what's underneath all that is anger. They're really angry that it's taken so long, or they're angry that it requires effort on their part.

There was a book years ago called *Feel the Fear and Do It Anyway*.[33] Well, that's what you've got to do. You've got to pull up your big girl panties and do it anyway. Because if you're just going to whine and bitch and moan, "Oh, this is too hard, I don't want to do it," then you need to go to acceptance. "OK. I'm just going to accept the fact that I'm going to die alone." Those are your options. Get over it and go do something, or accept the fact that this is your fate in life.

**Treva: You make your own luck by being proactive, putting forth effort, and having the right mindset?**

**Arielle:** You have to have patience and trust, while also being in action. At the same time you're in action, you simultaneously need to surrender and detach from how, when, and where it happens. The key is to know and trust that it's happening. This requires maturity and managing your monkey mind.

---

33   Susan Jeffers, *Feel the Fear and Do It Anyway* (Santa Monica, CA: Jeffers Press, 2007).

**Treva: What's more important: giving people hope for marriage, or giving them tools in the event they stay single?**

**Arielle:** Well, I don't have any tools for extended singlehood. It's something I don't believe in. If you want partnership, then that's possible. There are 7.5 billion people alive on the planet. Half of them are single, and half of that half are the opposite sex or whatever sex you want. So there's literally more than a billion possibilities.

And a lot of them are online, and looking for partnerships. Now yes, you do have to get good at sorting them, but what's possible is finding partnership. But it's not possible if you're not willing to do any work. And if you're not willing to do any work, then I'm the wrong person to talk to. You know, all I can see is possibility and where to go with the possibility.

## MY INTERVIEW WITH
## DR. KARIN ANDERSON ABRELL

Karin's journey to later-in-life wife was also about timing, being true to herself, and listening to the little voice inside her. Her story is typical of most women in their 20s, but with a twist.

**Treva: Tell me about your dating history.**

**Karin:** It starts out with a couple of boyfriends in college and then the typical experience in my 20s and 30s, with a dry spell in my 20s. That was before dating apps. You couldn't just pull out your phone and meet somebody on Tinder.

Because of the dry spell I started to doubt myself, as some single women do. If things aren't working out we assume maybe we're doing something wrong, and move from a confident posture into self-doubt. This leads me to my 30th birthday, and I meet a guy at a club in Chicago.

He was very accomplished, driven, kind, smart—great guy. On paper, a perfect match. We start dating, but even in the early stages, if I was honest with myself—which I wasn't prepared to be at that time—would have acknowledged that we didn't have that kind of chemistry that we all deeply desire. But

I'm 30 now, and my friends are married and starting to have families, so I kept on with a very good enough relationship until he proposed.

I was engaged for a year, and then two months before the wedding when I was 34, I became a runaway bride and called it off. I became more fearful of being in a mediocre relationship and living what I would have perceived as a lie. I became more afraid of that than being single.

**Treva: Do you identify as a late bloomer? You have been so focused and accomplished from an early age!**

**Karin:** Getting married at 42 is a late-blooming bride. In some ways, yes, and in some ways, I think I just didn't meet my person until I met my person. Yes, it took me a while, but it also shows that there's a quality of believing that the best is available in life, and I may have to be willing to wait for it. I'm willing to wait for something that is really special, rather than just how things come into place in the expected timeline.

I'm a fan of honoring your journey and your process and pace. And I do believe, sadly, many people try to force things to happen on the "expected" timeline, just so they can have the husband in place, the kids, keep up with the Joneses, keep up with their friends. So I really respect late bloomers because they are taking the harder route and hoping for the greater gain in the end.

**Treva: What kind of messages did you receive about marriage when you were growing up?**

**Karin:** I came from a very traditional family. My parents were together until my father passed away in 2016. My dad was the breadwinner and my mom never pumped gas in her car, and he didn't know how to use the washer and dryer. The message was "Marriage is forever," and I think they did have a really solid marriage, but there were times when I didn't see the amount of passion that I would've liked to have seen.

It was definitely something I was looking for, and again, it definitely compelled me to look at my relationship with my ex-fiancé and say, "I don't feel that passion and I definitely want that. I want that intense chemistry. I want to be with someone who we can't keep our hands off each other."

**Treva: What kind of messages did you grow up with about men specifically?**

**Karin:** I actually had very positive messages about men, that men were strong. Men stayed around. I believed that men could be good. And that's one of the things that kept me from settling.

**Treva: I think something happens when you're single a long time and endure a lot of heartbreak—your confidence erodes and your attachment style changes. What's your take on attachment styles?**

**Karin:** I definitely have a secure attachment style, but the School of Hard Knocks can really take you down. There were times when I got a little avoidant. Like when Dan asked to be exclusive, I had this sick to my stomach feeling because ever since I was 15 years old, every time I committed to someone and said, "Yes, let's be exclusive," it ended with a broken heart. I actually had to excuse myself and go to the bathroom, and I was like, "OK, calm down, Karin. You know, you gotta take the risk if you want the reward, right?"

**Treva: When you're single, not comparing yourself to others is easier said than done. I'd be at a friend's wedding, and the thought bubble over my head would say: "Why not me?" Does this sound familiar?**

**Karin:** Yeah, there were moments of "Ugh, I'm the single one at the wedding, yet again." There were times where I'd say to myself, "What does she got that I don't?" And there were times when I definitely didn't have it within myself to maintain hope.

I remember when I called off my engagement, and I was sobbing hysterically to my Maid of Honor, feeling like an utter disaster, and I just looked at her and said, "Heather, I just don't have any hope anymore. I just don't think love is going to be in the cards for me." And she said, "That's OK, Karin. I'll have hope for you."

**Treva: Wow. That's a great story! And that your friend knew instinctively what to say in that moment makes it all the more profound. Any advice for how other late bloomers can get through life's fragile moments?**

**Karin:** Surround yourself with people who can fill you up with hope and encouragement when it's too hard for you to do on your own.

**Treva: What was your learning curve on your journey to find love? Any mistakes or regrets?**

**Karin:** Yes, sure. There were times when I'd break up and not be able to work that person out of my system. I would vacillate between "We're totally broken up" and "We're kind of, I don't know, it's complicated." I would do that to myself, even when I was the one who cut it off initially. If you're going to lose something, do you want to lacerate it off in one fell swoop and dive head-first into the pain and agony, or do you want to drag it out for four years? Sadly, I did the latter too often.

**Treva: Can we talk about not having kids? I know this can be a sensitive issue, because—like me—you don't have kids. And you and I tried to conceive (unsuccessfully) later in life.**

**Karin:** Yeah, this is something that's not tidy for me. I don't have this all boxed up in a pretty package with a nice little tidy bow. It's still a pain point, something that I don't know that I'll ever fully understand. If you and I kept going into it, I'd be in tears, in like five minutes.

There's a choice every day to ask: Do I want to focus on what I don't have in my life and obsess about it and be angry about it and get myself tied up in knots about it, or do I want to acknowledge all of these other wonderful things in my life?

When I'm with friends, there's a lot of talk about kids because that's a very key element of their existence and their identity and what they're doing in this life. They're mothers, and I don't know if there's a more elevated and admired and valued role in our society than motherhood, so, I do feel like I missed out. I feel a little jealous of people who were able to have that kid in their timeline.

Dan and I got married when I was 42 and so we tried, because he'd had a vasectomy. He went to get it reversed, and the doctors said, "Well, you should probably just go straight to IVF because your wife's 42." So we went to Chicago, had the best IVF doctors, blah, blah, blah—and you know, because you went through it. And sometimes it just doesn't work.

I'm sure people will be like, "Well she's out of touch with her profound pain and loss," and you know, maybe I am, but I'm happier this way than obsessing about what I don't have every day of my life.

**Treva: At 50, I resigned myself to never getting married and having children. As hard as it was, I had to have that conversation with myself. Did you have a similar experience?**

**Karin:** There was a time when I thought I'm just unlucky in love. Some people meet the love of their lives and others don't, and I guess I'm just gonna be one of those people who doesn't.

And I'd say that over and over until I realized that that was a prison I was creating in my mindset, and I was creating that prison, making that my reality. And because I wasn't capable at that time of really challenging those thoughts and putting them in a positive light, I just started listening to people who were hopeful and positive.

They changed my thinking to "Any man who hasn't stayed around for me wasn't my person. Why would I ever want to be with someone who I had to beg to stay? No. I want someone who'd never let me get away."

When I started fully embracing it and believing it, my energy changed, and I'd go on dates with a different vibe.

**Treva: I think late bloomers are pros at waiting and being patient. Yet I know a lot of them struggle with the idea of being "late." Any advice on that front?**

**Karin:** Believe that being a late bloomer is a bonus. It's hard to see that because there's so much single shaming, but I think we have a beautiful advantage of having all those years of being independent, and all those skills that we developed, we bring into our marriages. I think our marriages are stronger and healthier and more fulfilling because of it.

**Treva: What's more important: giving people hope for marriage, or giving them tools in the event they stay single?**

**Karin:** The practical part of me says it's the tools for how to truly love and thrive in our single season, not seeing ourselves as second-class citizens. Not seeing this season as just waiting. I even hate the term "while you're waiting for the one."

You're not a lady-in-waiting. I talk about that in my book. You are thriving in your fullness of yourself. And I'm very passionate about trying to help them embrace their single season, because there's so many beautiful portions of their personality that they develop as a single woman that they really can't develop in partnership. I stand by that. I know people probably take issue with that, but I stand by it.

**Treva: Do you believe there's someone for everyone?**

**Karin:** I do, but I've got a client right now who's really wrestling with it. She's 44 and she's like, "I need to wrap my mind around the fact there may not be someone for me."

This resonated because I was that woman. I wrestled with it and had to wrap my head around it and make peace, just like her client. "There may not be someone for me" was cold hard truth, but as we know, the truth shall set you free.

My eternally optimistic and deeply romantic side wants to believe there is someone for everyone, and with a little work, preparation, and divine timing, it's possible. I've seen it happen. But the realistic side of me, the one that lived many years as a single person, has to be truthful. I had to be truthful back then, it's my duty now as a coach, to be just as truthful.

**Treva: Did you get to a point where you made peace with being single forever?**

**Karin:** I think the way I finally made peace was that I always believed in myself, and knew I was going to be OK either way. And that was really critical for me. Even if I didn't meet my person, I wasn't going to be the old, miserable single woman who's angry at the world and hates men.

—

As I ended my conversations with Arielle and Karin, I had a realization: To know you're going to be OK either way is everything.

## NINETEEN

# WHEREVER LIFE PLANTS YOU, BLOOM WITH GRACE

*The last to bloom is the strongest.*

—Rune Lazuli

With everything I now know about life and love, I still ponder these questions: Make it happen or let it happen? Have a plan or let things unfold? Hold on or let go? I think it's a little of all three.

This is my philosophy as a late bloomer, coach, and fitness pro. I know that getting what you want takes effort, getting it right takes practice, and not getting it at all takes acceptance.

To my fellow late bloomers, don't ever feel bad about getting a late start. Don't let society dictate your benchmarks or milestones. Your timeline is yours and yours alone, and you'll bloom when you're ready.

As I can attest, life doesn't come with a grand plan, but if you've got one, follow it. You don't need a vision of your future, but if you see it, keep it in your mind's eye. You don't need a road map, but if you have life GPS, use it. The only thing you need is to be proactive. So start *now*. Go *now*. Launch *now*. Reinvent *now*. Bloom *now*. Envision the person you want to be and go be it.

Remember, it's never too late and you're never too old to win a Pulitzer, become a famous painter, or open a chain of fried chicken franchises.

As self-help author Napoleon Hill once said: "Do not wait; the time will never be 'just right.' Start where you stand, and work with whatever tools you may have at your command, and better tools will be found as you go along."[34]

## DON'T WAIT TO CELEBRATE

As a coach, I believe there's strength in the struggle, but I also believe there's strength in having faith. Not the religious kind, not even the spiritual kind, but the kind that reminds you that if you don't lose another pound, fit into your jeans, get married or remarried, or have abs of steel, you'll live.

Being single takes faith. Faith that your person is out there, that finding The One is a real possibility. Without faith, why date? Why swipe? Why bother? But there's another kind of faith required to be single: faith that you're going to be just fine being single.

As a woman who spent 51 years alternating between avoiding love and working way too hard for it, here's my advice: Let go and let love find you.

You can achieve many things by the sweat of your brow, just not love. Love doesn't care how driven or goal-oriented you are. The only thing love cares about is that you make an effort and stay open to the possibilities. Stay open to whatever the universe brings, and do your part to welcome it in.

Stay open to divine timing, kismet, fate, serendipity, the chance encounter, and Jewish "bashert," the preordained or inevitable. Stay open to signs and signals.

---

34   Jeff Haden, "43 Best Napolean Hill Quotes," Inc.com, https://www.inc.com/jeff-haden/43-best-napoleon-hill-quotes-to-inspire-success-in-life-business.html (accessed June 9, 2022).

Stay open to love arriving late and not in the way you imagined. Because it might. Love might come in the form of an old friend, a former flame, or a high school crush. Love might come in the form of someone who's not your type, culture, or geographical preference. Don't count them out, don't be so quick to say no.

If you're of little faith and doubt any of what I'm telling you, read the *New York Times* mini-vows section and your faith will be restored. As one featured 89-year-old second-time bride reminds us: "Love is timeless. It can reach out to you at any age."

The only thing I'd advise is to prepare for love's arrival by being content without it. Do everything in your power to be the most content single person you can be because the more content you are being single, chances are, you won't be single for long.

When I was single, I had bottles of champagne in my refrigerator given to me as birthday gifts, hostess gifts, etc.: Veuve Clicquot, Dom Perignon, the good stuff. They sat in there for years unopened because I kept waiting for the "right time" to open them. I kept waiting for something to celebrate, something great to happen before I popped the cork.

During this time, I was training a client who owned a winery in Napa Valley. When I told her about stockpiling my champagne, she said: "You know champagne loses its fizz after a while. You really should drink it." I didn't believe her, so I went home and tested her theory. I reluctantly opened a bottle (I almost felt guilty doing it), and lo and behold, it was flat. I opened another. And another. After emptying six bottles of very expensive but very flat champagne down the sink, an epiphany bubbled up:

*I was waiting to be happy before I could celebrate.*

This epiphany stayed with me all these years, and as a result, I don't wait anymore. Even when I had no husband, boyfriend, dates, or prospects, I found things to celebrate.

So stop worrying about finding a partner, spouse, boyfriend, or girlfriend, and putting off your happiness because of it. Stop waiting to get in shape, get married, or make money before you can be happy. Stop letting the scale or your relationship status define you. And stop thinking you have to be perfect in order to meet your person.

Open that bottle of champagne right now and celebrate who you are, as you are. The truth is, this might be as good as it gets, so you better start enjoying it.

Getting married was a celebration for sure, but it was also a reality check for me. Newsflash: Marriage doesn't suddenly repair what's broken or fill what's empty if you're not already whole or fulfilled to begin with. That's your job. With a partner, you may get help around the house or a guy to help fix shit, but when it comes to running the business of your well-being or managing your self-esteem, you are the boss.

As I've discovered, marriage is as much about giving up control as it is about collaboration—not an easy concept for this fiercely autonomous Aquarian, who never asks for help, and does everything herself, including fixing shit around the house.

You know what's another reality check? Menopause (and going through it with someone you love).

**Marriage doesn't suddenly repair what's broken or fill what's empty if you're not already whole or fulfilled to begin with.**

## MENOPAUSE: THE STRUGGLE IS REAL

Nothing has fucked more with my head or my soul than menopause, and not because of the hormonal hell it is, but because it marked the official end to my fertility and any chance of having a baby with my own eggs.

Most women are happy to see their periods go. No more tampons, pads, PMS, cramps, or accidents. Not me. I loved my period. I even loved happening upon a bloody mess in my underwear, especially in my mid-40s, when I was hanging on to every period, and every cycle. Getting my period was monthly reassurance that I could still conceive, and my body's way of telling me it was still there for me.

Getting my period meant more than having a functioning system; it meant there was still hope. So when I went into perimenopause and my cycle became erratic, I knew the end was near. Losing my period wasn't freedom, it was failure.

When I first started dating Robby, every time we had sex, I secretly hoped I'd get pregnant and have a miracle menopause baby. I was on a last-ditch kamikaze mission to get knocked up, so I kept my fingers crossed and my legs open, but month after month, there was no pregnancy. I could hear Mother Nature whispering to me: "You're S.O.L," and Seinfeld's Soup Nazi shouting: "No baby for you!"

Menopause was the final nail. No more time on the clock. Game over. We could've adopted, but neither of us were interested in going that route, so we both decided to move forward as a child-free couple. The Rolling Stones' song "You Can't Always Get What You Want" said it all. I didn't get a baby, but I ended up getting what I needed: an adorable bouncing babe of a husband.

Getting married for the first time in midlife is weird, but so is being middle-aged. If you've been single for as long as Robby and me, it's easy to forget how old you are. You're still sort of living the same life you did at 30, with the same freedom, but no growing kids to mark time. You're sort of in a time warp.

At least my friends and I all went into menopause together—except I went into it walking down the aisle, and got my first hot flash on my honeymoon. Hitting midlife is surreal. Your hair gets thinner, your middle gets thicker; what was once tight is loose, what was firm is soft. It's a total mindfuck. Your body morphs right before your eyes—oh, and your eyes go too. I need glasses for everything now, and maybe that's a good thing, since I can't see my wrinkles. The first time I farted when I laughed, I knew middle age was upon me.

You either have high cholesterol or low T. You may play hard, but you pay for it the next day. Our medicine chest is filled with Aleve, and ice packs outnumber frozen food in our freezer. Your memory isn't what it used to be either. I'd go into more detail on this, but I just forgot what I was going to say.

Another weird thing about getting married older is being in a bridal salon dressing room surrounded by girls half your age. They're young, with perky boobs, and I'm as old as dirt with tits down to the ground. By the way, if it's been a while since you've been in a bridal salon, let me bring you up to speed: Every gown looks like it could be from a Kardashian closet.

I remember looking at my fellow brides in the dressing room, musing wistfully: *You have your whole life ahead of you, and I've already lived half of mine. You're young and innocent, and I'm old and jaded. You're probably going to get*

*pregnant in a few months, and I'm menopausal. And we're all getting married,*
*bitches, so haha!*

## MIDLIFE LOVE: A WHOLE NEW OPERATING SYSTEM

Getting together in midlife has its challenges. I have my system; Robby has his. I'm a creature of habit; so is he. He stockpiles; I throw it out. He buys in bulk; I shop for a day. He's a micromanager, and I can manage quite fine, thank you very much. We're both dug in, strong-willed, and set in our ways.

The biggest fights Robby and I have are about flexibility, patience, and compromise—things that don't come easy when you're older or have been single for a long time. Anyone who got married young sort of grows up with their spouse. You form your systems, values, and opinions together, and see the world through the same eyes. But when you get together later in life, it's like learning a whole new operating system—or at least upgrading the software to make it compatible.

It's also a whole new language. In fact, love is a language that everyone speaks differently. I discovered this when I heard about *The Five Love Languages: How to Express Heartfelt Commitment to Your Mate*, the bestselling book by Dr. Gary Chapman.

The five love languages are five distinct areas through which we give and receive love, and how we communicate and express our needs:[35]

1. **Words of affirmation**: Listening, encouraging, and building up our partner through compliments and other verbal reminders.

2. **Quality time**: Spending time with your partner and giving them your undivided attention without distraction.

---

35   Chapman explains the five love languages in a series of videos here: https://5lovelanguages.com/learn (accessed June 28, 2022).

3. **Physical touch**: Demonstrating that you care through varying degrees of physical intimacy and touch. Nonverbal body language includes hugs, kisses, caresses, and sex.

4. **Acts of service**: Doing something on behalf of your partner you know they'll appreciate. Running errands, doing the shopping, helping with chores, making meals, are all acts of service.

5. **Receiving gifts**: Giving big or small thoughtful tokens of your appreciation.

When it comes to love, Robby and I are on the same page, but we speak different languages. I've determined that I'm a Words of Affirmation person, and he's an Acts of Service guy. I like verbal affirmation, and Robby likes thoughtful gestures. For example, I like to tell him how brilliant and handsome he is (Words of Affirmation), and he likes to bring me flowers for no reason (Act of Service). Our new goal is to teach ourselves to speak each other's language. For example, he'll tell me how good this book is (Words of Affirmation) and I'll blow him in return (Act of Service).

Even though I'm married, life is still pretty much the same. My issues, worries, fears, and responsibilities haven't magically gone away. There's still debt to pay down, a business to run, clients to coach, aging parents to care for, and a future to plan. Plus, I still need to learn how to fold a fitted sheet and bake a turkey.

**The journey isn't over, and I've got more blooming to do.**

I struggle with my changing body, growing old gracefully, and resisting plastic surgery (although I can't make any promises that I'll resist forever). The self-care never stops—especially now that I'm a wife and partner, I have even more incentive to care for myself.

I didn't come this far just to come this far. The journey isn't over, and I've got more blooming to do.

# TWENTY

# LOVE AND LOSS IN THE TIME OF CORONAVIRUS

*It doesn't matter what you bear, but how you bear it.*

—Seneca

As I was bringing this book to a close, 2020 hit, and hit hard. In less than a year both of my parents died, and the coronavirus pandemic swept the planet.

It was a one-two punch. My "parental" pandemic started in December of 2019, when both my mom and dad coincidentally landed at Cedars Sinai hospital within a week of each other. Mom was rushed to the ER with complications from unmanaged Type 1 diabetes, and Dad got a lung cancer diagnosis that metastasized to his brain. His situation was terminal; hers was bleak but survivable.

Dad was a 91-year-old chain smoker, so we knew at some point all those cigarettes would catch up with him. And they did.

After spending a week at the hospital conferring with his doctors, his wife Suzanne and my stepsister Stacy, he decided he wanted to go sooner rather than later. He probably only had a few weeks to live but didn't want to prolong the inevitable; he wanted to end his life, on his terms, with dignity. This meant assisted suicide. It was his wish, not mine. I knew in my heart it was the best thing for him, and I had to honor it.

So we started the process: ordering the drugs, getting doctors' approvals, hiring hospice nurses, and setting up a hospital bed at home. Then we had to endure the 14-day waiting process that requires more signatures, and visits from doctors to confirm he was of sound mind and ready to die.

Death with dignity isn't just brave for the dying patient—it's brave for everyone involved.

Robby, Suzanne, Stacy, and I were all on rotation, making daily and hourly visits, sitting at his bedside, holding his hand. His time was short, and every day had become precious. We all had to stay strong, which was no easy task. Knowing he had an expiration date was heavy, and it made it hard to keep a smile on my face when I'd see him. After every visit when I'd say goodbye, he would kiss my hand, and then I'd wait till I was in my car before bursting into tears.

Mom, meanwhile, was still in the ICU enduring a litany of health problems, including diabetic ketoacidosis, pneumonia, a pulmonary embolism, and sepsis. Robby and I were ping-ponging back and forth between her and my dad every day for weeks. To say we were on death watch would be an understatement; to say I was on adrenaline autopilot would be putting it lightly.

The end-of-life medication arrived via FedEx, and again, Dad was asked if he wanted to go through with it. He said "Yes" emphatically, and the plans were put into motion. He chose January 21, 2020.

We all congregated that day at his bedside along with the hospice nurse and chaplain. Two "cocktails" were administered in succession: The first one stopped his heart, and the more potent second potion took him to "Cloud City," as he often referred to heaven.

We surrounded him in a circle of courage, staying as stoic as we could. We said our quiet goodbyes and watched him take his last breath. The whole process took a couple of hours and was the most surreal thing I've ever witnessed.

It's strange knowing someone's expiration date, knowing exactly when they're going to die. We schedule births, but we never schedule deaths. I know it brings families great comfort to see their loved ones end their pain and suffering, but for me, I'm not sure it brought me the closure or comfort I was hoping for.

What happened after was not the emotion I was expecting. Robby and I went to get dinner, but as soon as we entered the restaurant, I lost my appetite. A wave of panic came over me; I got nauseous, anxious, and my heart started racing. I excused myself from the table and went outside to get some air because I was about to pass out.

While outside, something occurred to me: This feeling was familiar. *I knew this feeling*. I had experienced it before but couldn't place it. Then it hit me: It was the same feeling I used to get when a guy broke up with me. The same anxiety, the same knot in my stomach. Like most breakups, this loss of my father was final. There was no changing his mind, no second thoughts, no fighting for me. He was done and gone.

*You can't go yet, there's so much more to say, I have more questions, there's more to do, more to talk about, more stuff to figure out and resolve,* is what ran through my head, as if I had said it a million times before. In the days after his death I couldn't eat, my hair fell out, and Ativan became my best friend again, just like it had after a breakup. Pot also became a good friend of mine again, but this time it came in the form of CBD tincture drops, which either hadn't been invented or weren't readily available the last time I'd gone through a breakup.

Even though I had many years with my father, and knew he was suffering, I still wanted him around a little longer. I wasn't ready to let go. We had unfinished business, or so I felt. And the feeling that he's not coming back, that I can never see him again, still grips me with a weird panic. Just writing about it makes me need to take a deep breath.

After my dad died, my mother was released from the hospital to a rehab facility, where she continued to convalesce. After three weeks at rehab we moved her into an assisted living facility, where she had a lovely studio apartment. Robby and I decorated it with new furniture and her own belongings, to make her feel at home. But three weeks into her stay, she fell and broke her hip. She was sent back to the hospital and ended up getting hip replacement surgery, which was subpar, because two months later, we got a call that her hip had come out of its socket.

I should mention she had no idea my father had passed, and we purposely kept it a secret, feeling the news would add unnecessary pressure to her fragile health.

Crisis mode and adrenaline autopilot continued. Dad was gone, and now it was Mom 24/7. Every day unidentified numbers would pop up on my phone, and I knew it was either a doctor, nurse, social worker, or case manager calling to give me some bad news, which would send my heart into my throat. When my mother finally died, I had to change my ringtone because the sound triggered such intense PTSD.

Mom didn't go quickly like my father. Sonjia Brandon had more living to do, and there was no way she was going out without a fight. And fight she did, for another three months, in and out of acute care facilities, hospitals, emergency rooms, ICUs, and nursing homes, always hanging on by a thread. With my mother's big ego, I used to joke that she was too vain to die.

## LIFE AND DEATH UNDER LOCKDOWN

In early March of 2020, just after her hip surgery, we started hearing about a strange flu called the coronavirus from China, which was making its way into the US and spreading fast. In a matter of weeks, it became a full-blown pandemic. On March 16, all eldercare facilities were put on lockdown. We were *all* on lockdown.

She finally passed on May 8, 2020, in a nursing home, all alone, with no family surrounding her, no circle of courage, no one to hold her hand.

All said and done, between December and May she had been in 14 different hospital beds, and because of the pandemic, I wasn't able to see her for the last three months of her life. The phone call came early one morning from the nursing home telling me she had passed. After giving me their condolences, they promptly asked when the cremation service was coming to pick up her body because they needed more beds.

Because of COVID-19, outside of the entertainment trade papers and *Los Angeles Times* obituaries, there was no official goodbye, proper funeral, or memorial. She just slipped away quietly to the big commercial agency in the sky—which wasn't like her at all, since she loved a big entrance and making an even bigger exit. It was an inglorious end to a big life, an unfair send-off for someone who'd been such a force for so many people, including clients, associates, colleagues, her family—and me, especially.

Like so many other tough moments in my life that I handled alone, I could've done the same here; but luckily, I had Robby. He was now my family, my circle of courage, and he held my hand throughout the entire ordeal.

After my father passed, I didn't have much time to grieve since I was still on death watch with my mom. And maybe that was a good thing. I was too busy to take in the enormity of what I had just witnessed: my father dying right in front of my eyes. When Mom went I thought I'd get some closure, or relief, or go into a period of tearful mourning. But that didn't happen.

Instead, I was struck again with the most intense separation anxiety, almost worse than when my father passed. So intense, I literally couldn't breathe. Normally one's eyes would be swollen shut from crying. Not mine. I was too busy trying to get my heart out of my throat to shed a tear or take a breath. Even though we were very different, we were still very close, and in this moment, I realized just how karmically connected we were.

It also confirmed just how karmically connected my parents were. One couldn't help but to marvel at the fact they went out together. Coincidence? I think not. Even though they had zero communication in the final months, I think they both knew. Besides, there was no way my mother was going to let my father go anywhere without her.

If you couldn't tell by now, my mother loomed very large in my life, and her impact on me cannot be overstated. You can hear her voice in my voice and feel her presence throughout this book. Growing up, and into adulthood, we had our share of problems. We fought, argued, and thought we knew better for each other. To some degree I know that all mother–daughter relationships are fraught with some conflict; ours was fraught with plenty.

She took up a lot of emotional real estate. She could be demanding and exacting, and many times I didn't know how to say "no" to her (remember, I had no boundaries). Her problems became my problems, my problems became her

## I didn't just lose a parent, I lost a very codependent part of me.

problems. And so it went. When she went, I didn't just lose a parent, I lost a very codependent part of me. I felt like I had a phantom amputated limb—even when it's gone, it still feels like it's there.

A few weeks after her passing, when George Floyd was killed—which set off riots, looting, and violence across the country—my healing became all but impossible. With everything that happened in 2020—parents, civil unrest, political strife, raging wildfires near us in California, a raging virus, and my overwhelming sadness at the state of our country—there wasn't much of a chance to decompress and recover. Who could? We were all on a heightened state of alert. And with a raging pandemic going on, we were all on death watch.

I was completely unprepared to lose both parents within four months of each other; I was ill-equipped to deal with the emotional fallout; I was terrified of getting COVID; and terrified our country was spiraling toward a civil war, especially after the armed insurrection at the Capitol on January 6, 2021. I still fear for our country because now it's democracy that's hanging by a thread. With everything going on, it became painfully clear that my healing would have to wait.

Robby and I hunkered down and sheltered in place. The shutdown—for better or for worse—forced me to reflect and be alone with my thoughts, which were deep, and at times dark.

Here's what became clear: I'm an orphan now. No kids, no siblings . . . who will take care of me when I get old?

Suddenly, the sorrow of not having children began to haunt me again. It was like grieving a third loss, after my mom and dad. I thought I had processed it years ago; I thought I had turned the page on motherhood, but here it was, alive and well and torturing me with new regret. I was sad all over again.

To make matters worse, all my anxious attachment issues came roaring back. *What if something happens to Robby? What if I lose him? What if he gets sick? What if he leaves?* What if . . . what if . . . what if . . .

I found myself gripped with insecurity and needing reassurance. I became so dependent and clingy that I didn't even recognize myself. Who was this strong woman who was so needy and fragile?

I was so afraid of being a burden on Robby, but he was undaunted. He rose to the occasion as a husband and son-in-law in every way. He helped with my parents' affairs, handled legal matters, and did the grocery shopping. He even colored my hair when I was too scared to leave the house to go to the salon. So many times I wanted to call my parents to tell them what a great job he was doing, but then I remembered they were dead and I couldn't call. My only hope was that they were looking down from heaven and seeing it for themselves.

## VULNERABILITY IS SCARY AF

I know I've mentioned many times in this book how I knew Robby was a good man, but after this experience, it's now confirmed. A good man, as I've seen, will accept you and your attachment style, be with you in the darkness, hold your hand, and walk you through the scary parts.

In the darkness, I would remember the old saying, "'Tis better to have loved and lost, than never to have loved at all."

Except in my mind, I changed it to: What if it's easier to have never loved at all than to lose the love you had?

I can see why people with anxious or avoidant attachment styles opt out of love altogether. The pain and heartbreak can be too much, so why attach in the first place?

Those moments left me feeling extremely vulnerable, which, despite how much I like it for my clients, I don't like it for myself. I don't care what Brené Brown says. Vulnerability is scary AF.

I've got this pedigree of strength and power, so this shouldn't happen, I thought. I'm the badass, tough-as-nails fitness pro, the woman who embodies self-sufficiency, and the life coach who preaches empowerment, and yet here I was, unable to practice anything I preached.

All those months of being on adrenaline autopilot while trying to outrun a raging pandemic, plus all the prior years of carrying my parents' emotional load, finally did me in. I crashed.

Suddenly, everything hurt and exhausted me. Every muscle and bone ached. Even my hair hurt. I had no stamina, no endurance, and even the littlest task overwhelmed me. I pulled both hamstrings; developed Achilles tendonitis, excruciating TMJ, and "frozen shoulder"; and couldn't lift my left arm for six months. Then there were the days I couldn't get out of bed. I forgot I'd been a competitive athlete once, which depressed me even more. For the first time, I really felt my age. No, actually I really felt old.

To make matters worse, I was hit with a second-wave menopausal blast—with joint pain, anxiety, and night sweats—that blew out whatever little wind was remaining in my sails.

These inexplicable aches and pains and bizarre symptoms were my undoing, and it felt like my body was betraying me. Not only was I a physical wreck, I felt like I'd aged 150 years in little more than 12 months and looked every minute of it. Robby assured me this wasn't the case (Words of Affirmation just when I needed them).

The healing process was once again delayed as my father-in-law, Eddie Scharf, Robby's best friend and best man, passed away in the middle of all this, in March 2021, at age 99. This time, I was there to hold Robby's hand in case he became clingy and dependent, which he didn't. He stayed remarkably strong.

Even though Eddie lived the last 12 years of his life in Todos Santos in Baja, Mexico, Robby made sure he called him practically every day at 5:30 p.m. (and recorded many of them). I loved hearing and being part of their lovefest in every call. Robby would grieve after many of these calls, knowing there wasn't going to be an endless supply of them.

Robby and Eddie's relationship was easy and uncomplicated, with everything said and understood by the time he died. Mine, not so much. My relationship with my parents was complicated, and so was my grief.

"Complicated grief," as defined by the Mayo Clinic, is when the painful emotions of a loved one's death are so severe that you have trouble recovering and resuming normal life.[36] It's like being in an ongoing, heightened state of

---

36   "Complicated Grief," Mayo Clinic, https://www.mayoclinic.org/diseases-conditions/complicated-grief/symptoms-causes/syc-20360374 (accessed June 9, 2022).

mourning that keeps you from healing. *It also occurs more often in females and with older age* (WTF! I can't get a break!).

There are many factors that increase the risk of developing complicated grief, but the one that hit closest to home for me was "separation anxiety," which makes sense because I have a history of it. When you have a harder time detaching, it's harder to unpack and sort through your emotions. I can see why they call healing "a process," because it takes time and work, and I'm a work in progress.

# Let Go Like a Pro

I'm no bereavement expert; I'm just a daughter who got her ass handed to her when her parents died. For this reason, I feel qualified to share some things I did (and wish I had done) before my parents passed away. As your parents age, keep these things in mind:

- If you haven't already, record their voices.
- After they pass, don't sell, give away, or donate their clothes or belongings too fast. Sit with it for a while, then decide. I sold some of my mother's designer items too quickly to a high-end resale company, and immediately regretted it. When I tried to buy them back, they refused.
- Start forgiving your parents and releasing your anger while they're still alive.
- Find a therapist for support and guidance now. Don't wait till they're gone.
- Thank them for what they taught you, and never stop thanking them.
- Visualize life after parents. What do you want to accomplish? What kind of legacy do you want to be?
- Make peace and come to terms now.

After all the tragedy and crises I experienced in 2020, a crisis even more traumatic happened: I found my first gray pube. Actually, it was Robby who found it, since as you know, he's down there on the regular. Regardless, it was devastating, and I'm still recovering. I know that the death of a loved one—particularly a parent—can make you ponder your own aging and mortality; I just never thought I'd be pondering it through my vagina.

# A FINAL WORD
# ON BLOOMING AND
# BECOMING

*It takes courage to grow up and become who you really are.*

—e. e. cummings

From releasing my death grip on marriage, to letting go of my parents, to saying goodbye to my youth and fertility, I've realized more and more that surrender isn't just a last resort, it's a superpower. Surrender was my superpower when I was single, and I'm calling upon it now to get me through this period of my life.

This time, though, surrender looks different, and means more. This version of surrender means being content with whatever I can achieve, satisfied with less-than-maximum output, OK with less-than-stellar performance, and grateful for the small wins. I told you in the introduction that I was deeply human, and now I'm more so—and I'm surrendering to that too.

As an athlete, I've asked a lot of my body over the years; now, I'm asking my body to go slow and have patience with me. My high demands are more forgiving, and my expectations are more reasonable. Things have changed; so have I.

Don't worry—I haven't gone totally soft. I'm still a self-improvement junkie. I still love the sweat. I still dig discipline and hard work. Effort will always turn me on, and aiming high is hot. Transformation thrills me to no end. I still believe there's strength in the struggle, but I also believe there's strength in self-acceptance.

## SELF-ACCEPTANCE IS THE NEW BLACK

My new strength is letting go of control. My strength is being vulnerable. My new strength is *not* being strong. I've had to swallow some tough pills in my day, but that one's a doozy.

Gulp.

Self-improvement is sexy, but self-acceptance is the new black.

When you accept yourself, you tell the world you're a badass who can't be messed with. You tell the world you're comfortable in your skin and grounded in the rest of you. When you accept yourself, you tell everyone, "I am enough just as I am," and if there is a desire to improve it comes from a healthy, self-loving place that wants to achieve its potential, not punish itself for not being perfect. And lest I remind you again, there is no such thing as perfection anyway, so stop trying. And looking. It doesn't exist.

As Robby wrote earlier, sometimes "good enough" *is* good enough, as our podcast guest Lori Gottlieb told us on the show. And sometimes, self-acceptance *is* self-improvement.

Remember my five indicators of success? Indicator #5 is having a measure of self-worth. As a coach, clients come to me all the time with good intentions to change, and I'm here to assist. However, if a client doesn't think they deserve a great love, job, body, or life to begin with, it'll be an uphill climb for them, and a tougher job for me.

There's another aspect of self-improvement I need to address: external challenges.

When you're struggling to keep your job, make ends meet, get enough sleep, or survive a pandemic, it's hard to think about leveling up. Many people can't afford fancy gyms or expensive diet plans; some can't even afford healthcare. I know I've talked about the importance of "doing the work," but sometimes doing the work is just getting out of bed and getting through the day.

When I talk about self-improvement, I'm talking about doing what you can in your power. Using what's at your disposal. Getting resourceful. Being conscious. Using your free will to make healthy choices. Making the best of a situation. Working with what you've got. Controlling what you can, and letting the rest go. Honoring your highest good. Not comparing your life to Instagram. Do this, and you're already improving.

I put all this into action when I felt my world was falling apart and was racked with injuries and fatigue. Because I couldn't exercise and wasn't getting my usual fix of endorphins, I went into an even deeper funk. Exercise keeps me sane; it's necessary medication for my mental health and psyche. Without it I'm a mess, so in its place, I did what I could to feel better: I meditated, journaled, played online Scrabble, mah-jongg, and watched the reboot of *Sex and the City*. On good days, when I had energy, I played tennis, albeit not well.

I also prayed a lot for mercy.

## GO SMALL OR GO HOME

When my injuries started to finally heal and my pain started to ease, I slowly ventured out. At first, it was walking around the block, or riding a few minutes with the Peloton app on an old, pre-owned Schwinn commercial spinning bike I bought during the pandemic. *Baby steps.* I started exercising once a week, then increased to twice a week. *Small victory.* I upped my intensity by including more challenging workouts when my body allowed. *Minor achievement.* Just as I'd get some momentum, though, grief would tap me on the shoulder, my body would start aching again, the sadness would set back in, and I'd have to start all over.

Operative words here being "When my body allowed," which is now my new mantra. When my body allowed, I'd hit the restart button, put my sneakers back on, and remember what educator Jaime Escalante said in the movie *Stand and*

*Deliver*: "Life is not about how many times you fall down. It's about how many times you get back up."

I had just gotten back up for what felt like the umpteenth time, when something else tapped me on the shoulder: COVID. After two and half years of what felt like running from the law, both Robby and I tested positive. Robby had it worse, but the terror of finally getting it made it far worse for me. When I saw that home test result, I flew into a total panic, as all those horrifying past scenes and stories of sick and dying people became my reality. As it turned out, the fear was worse than the virus. My case was mild but let me be clear: This thing is no joke. COVID is very, very contagious. So contagious, in fact, that I'm now convinced it comes out of your eyeballs.

As I recovered, I remembered Jaime Escalante's words and did what any author with a book to publish would do: I got back up, put my sneakers on, hit the restart button, and brought this baby to a close.

## Reboot Like a Pro

If you're coming back from an injury, an illness, recovering from a setback, or healing from heartbreak, here are some fitness-inspired tips to reboot:

- Listen to your body and have patience with it.
- "Start slow and taper off," as the old runners' slogan goes.
- Focus on small achievable steps, and don't get overwhelmed by the whole journey.
- Don't compare yourself to your younger self. Be content with who you are, and what you can do now.
- Hit the restart button as much as you need.
- Don't expect to break land speed records or hit your personal best every time.
- For Type A people: you can push yourself—just don't kill yourself.

## YOU WILL SUCCEED

After everything we've talked about in this book—empowerment, improvement, and acceptance—I know you will succeed. I know because you've gotten this far in the book. I know because you have a burning desire to change, you're committed to the process, you believe you're capable, you're not afraid of a little pain, and you feel worthy.

So keep going, keep moving, and keep being your bad self, because you can't keep a late bloomer or a good woman down. And if someone says you can't do it, or you're too old, tell them to fuck off, and do it anyway.

I'm going to keep writing, coaching, helping people, imparting wisdom, and being my bad self along with you, because that's my calling. And by heeding the call, I will continue to honor my parents and my highest good.

> **If someone says you can't do it, or you're too old, tell them to fuck off, and do it anyway.**

I want to keep going and growing. I want to accept the aging process without fear and loathing, and I want to make the most of my second act with my husband by my side. Even with this old bod and gray pubes, I'm pressing on. As I said earlier, I have more blooming to do.

I have to remember I'm the person who ran five marathons, drives a stick shift in LA, and tried to get pregnant on her own—so if there was ever a time to put a lifetime of resilience to work, it's now.

It took me 51 years to get married, and I want this thing to last. Not that I think it won't, but because life is short, time is precious, and we got a late start; so I want to enjoy as many days as I can with Robby. I know there are no guarantees that anything in life lasts, so right now, I'm going to acknowledge the progress I've made and pop the cork. Better yet, I'm going to crack open that expensive bottle of reposado and celebrate. I found love, but I found myself first. That's reason to raise my glass and toast.

A shot of tequila to you and your journey: Be it now or later, you're blooming as you should.

L'Chaim, Motherfuckers!

# HIGHLIGHT REEL

The following is a highlight reel of *Done Being Single* episodes and guests. Links for all episodes can be found at www.donebeingsingle.com.

"Admit It, You Suck at Relationships," with Guy Finley, writer, philosopher, and spiritual leader, November 3, 2018.

"A Little Self-Help to Help Find Love," with Dr. Terry Simpson, psychologist and fitness professional, December 29, 2018.

"An Intimate Conversation with Stacey Nelkin," with Stacey Nelkin, actor and teacher, November 18, 2018.

"Are Men Still from Mars and Women from Venus?," with John Gray, relationship counselor and bestselling author, July 25, 2019.

"Are Politics Screwing with Your Love Life?," with John Mirish, Beverly Hills Council Member; Tania Bradkin, licensed clinical social worker; Richard Greene, attorney and communication strategist; and Sharon Appleman Greenwald, senior content writer, March 18, 2018.

"Are We Hardwired to Date a Certain Way?," with Dr. Duana Welch, professor, author, and dating coach, May 3, 2022.

"Attachment Theory: Your Missing Link to Love," with Gary Salyer, transformational relationship mentor and author, June 16, 2019.

"Bad Boys and Crazy Chicks," with Dale Archer, psychiatrist and radio/TV personality, June 16, 2018.

"Be a Master of Seduction," with Raj Persaud, psychiatrist and TED Talk speaker, September 20, 2019.

"Being Single and COVID-19: A Doctor and Dating Expert Speak," with Dr. Andre Berger, anti-aging expert; and Sandy Weiner, dating coach, March 20, 2020.

"Beware Dating Burnout and Bitterness," with Dr. Karin Anderson Abrell, psychology professor, podcaster, and author, February 21, 2020.

"Be Your Authentic Self Without Scaring People Away," with Madeline Charles, therapist and love coach, July 22, 2019.

"Be Your Own Happiness Boss," with Daryn Kagan, broadcast journalist; and Ricky Powell, author and business coach, May 5, 2018.

"Channel Your Inner Stud," with Spencer Burnett, business alchemist and relationship coach, May 15, 2019.

"Confessions of a Professional Wingman," with Thomas Edwards, dating coach and professional wingman, August 30, 2019.

"Conquering Betrayal," with Anita Chlipala, marriage and family therapist, April 30, 2019.

"Crazy for Chaos," with Judson Brewer, neuroscientist, psychiatrist, and bestselling author, November 22, 2019.

"Date Ready: From Manscaping to Anti-Aging," with Andre Berger, cosmetic surgeon; and Kimberly Seltzer, image consultant, June 9, 2018.

"Dating a Single Parent/Blending Families," with Monica Hurt, licensed marriage and family therapist, December 22, 2018.

"Dating Is a Numbers Game, Here's How to Play," with Mike Goldstein, men's relationship coach, June 4, 2019.

"Dating TMI: Let It Rip or Keep It Zipped?," with Gretchen Kubacky, health psychologist; and Bex Burton, love coach, July 14, 2018.

"Dating with Baggage," with Thomas Carouso, marriage and family therapist, April 7, 2018.

"Dating with Depression," with Catrien Villamil, licensed marriage and family therapist; and Sharon Appleman Greenwald, associate creative director, March 21, 2019.

"Deal Breakers: Dig Them or Ditch Them?," with Brian Howie, host of *The Great Love Debate* podcast, March 17, 2018.

"Divorce Pandemic-Style: What Every Couple Needs to Know," with James Sexton, attorney, June 18, 2020.

"Does Love Happen by Accident or On Purpose?," with Orna and Matthew Walters, soulmate coaches, October 20, 2018.

"Done Being an Idiot," with Larry Miller, comedian, January 10, 2019.

"Done with Dating," with Beth Cone Kramer, journalist and author, February 4, 2019.

"Don't Let a Tough Childhood Stop You from Finding Love," with Margaret Rutherford, psychologist and author; Joyce Robinson, actor and philanthropist; and Fredrica Duke, actor, writer, and filmmaker, May 12, 2018.

"Don't Let Dating Beat You!," with Gary Collins, author and digital nomad, August 9, 2019.

"Don't Take Dating So Damn Seriously!," with Craig Shoemaker, comedian, author, and writer, July 28, 2018.

"Everything You Wanted to Know About Sex but Were Afraid to Ask," with Lou Pagett, sex educator, June 30, 2018.

"Everything You Want Is on the Other Side of Fear," with Gay and Katie Hendricks, authors, teachers, and personal growth pioneers, June 23, 2018.

"Executive Coaching for Dating Success?," with Bill Hart, executive coach, March 8, 2019.

"Face It, You Need Therapy," with Jenny TeGrotenhuis, certified Gottman relationship therapist, December 6, 2019.

"Forget New Year's Resolutions, Make Valentine's Resolutions," with Ken Page, author and relationship expert, February 14, 2019.

"Get Rid of Dating Anxiety Once and for All," with Chris Rackliffe, mental health advocate and author, February 5, 2021.

"Getting to the Heart of Love and Loss," with Jonathon Aslay, midlife dating coach, February 7, 2020.

"Got Chemistry?," with Zannah Hackett, relationship technologist; Karen Page, psychic counselor; and Spencer Grendahl, astrologer, June 2, 2018.

"Hater to Dater in 60 Minutes Flat," with Susan Winter, bestselling author and love coach, August 15, 2019.

"How to Be a Confident MF'er," with David Snyder, confidence coach and neurolinguistic programming specialist practitioner, October 25, 2019.

"How to Date in a Feminist World," with Alex Williamson, chief brand officer for Bumble, July 21, 2018.

"How to Deal with Your Midlife Crisis," with Ada Calhoun, author, March 6, 2020.

"How to Get Past Your Past," with Guy Finley, self-realization author and teacher, January 10, 2020.

"Time to Kick the Sh*t Out of Your Inner Bully," with Theresa Byrne, martial arts expert and TED Talk speaker, February 28, 2020.

"How to Find Love While Finding Yourself," with Debi Carlin Boyle, health and fitness coach, February 14, 2020.

"How to Know When Someone's Lying," with Robin Dreeke, expert behavioral analyst and senior FBI agent, May 7, 2020.

"How to Know When You're Done," with Shannon Colleary, screenwriter and blogger, February 17, 2018.

"How to Slay Pandemic Anxiety," with Lisa Gornall, spiritual medium, mindset, and energy coach, August 21, 2020.

"How to Stop Chasing Love," with Dasha Schindler, author, December 16, 2020.

"I Love You, but I Hate Your Politics," with Jeanne Safer, author, September 5, 2019.

"I'm Doing Everything Right, So What's Going Wrong?," with Francesca Hogi, love coach and TV personality, October 6, 2019.

"Is 'Good Enough' Good Enough?," with Lori Gottlieb, psychotherapist, *New York Times* bestselling author, and advice columnist for *The Atlantic*, April 14, 2018.

"Is Love Written in the Stars?," with Carol Allen, astrologer, March 31, 2019.

"Is There Such a Thing As Right Person, Wrong Time?," with Karin Anderson Abrell, psychology professor and author, February 24, 2018.

"It's National Singles Day! Your Call to Action!," with Cheryl Besner, dating coach and matchmaker; Kristen Manieri, certified habits coach; and Tai Tran, founder of Blue dating app, September 22, 2018.

"Keeping Sex Alive and Well During COVID," with Susan Bratton, intimacy expert, CEO of Personal Life Media, March 9, 2019.

"Keep Married Sex Alive!," with Susan and Tim Bratton, sexperts and hot married couple, November 3, 2019.

"Let That Sh*t Go, Let Love In," with Gay Hendricks, author and coach, October 13, 2018.

"Let Your Freak Flag Fly!," with Carol and David of *The Sexy Lifestyle* podcast, December 15, 2018.

"Look for a House Like You Would a Spouse," with Brian Belefant, real estate broker and author, July 24, 2020.

"Looking for a Few Good Men?," with Lisa Copeland, midlife dating coach, December 8, 2018.

"Looks Aren't Everything, but They Matter," with Kim Seltzer, image consultant; and Jill Brown, fitness professional, July 17, 2019.

"Love and Money," with Kine Corder, financial expert, April 11, 2019.

"Love & Politics: The State of the Union," with Jeanne Safer, psychologist and author; and Richard Brookheiser, political journalist for *The National Review*, September 18, 2020.

"Love, British Style," with Nichi Hodgson, British journalist, April 24, 2019.

"Loving with Sobriety," with Robert Navarro, certified Gottman therapist and presenter, July 6, 2020.

"Making the Case for Dating Age-Appropriate Women," with Jillian Franklyn, author and writer; and Allison Cane, professional photographer, December 12, 2019.

"Mars & Venus Quarantined with John Gray," with John Gray, relationship counselor and author, April 16, 2020.

"Mastering Chaos," with Phil Morris, actor, March 27, 2020.

"Meet the New Post-Pandemic You," with Jill Brown, fitness expert, June 10, 2021.

"Men, Is Your Heart Talking to Your Other Parts?," with Jayson Gaddis, author, relationship expert, and coach, June 7, 2022.

"Men, What Say You?," with anonymous single guys, September 1, 2018.

"Nobody's Perfect: Are You Too Picky or Not Picky Enough?," with Renee Piane, love designer; and Allana Pratt, intimacy expert, March 10, 2018.

"Older & Wiser: How to Find Love Later in Life," with *Done Being Single* co-hosts Treva Scharf and Robby Scharf, May 28, 2019.

"Older Women/Younger Men, Why the Hell Not?," with Vicki Larson, journalist and author, September 3, 2020.

"Online Dating: Are You a Pro or a Con?," with Julie Spira, online dating expert, author, and media personality, March 24, 2018.

"Perfectly Hidden Depression," with Dr. Margaret Rutherford, clinical psychologist and author, June 25, 2020.

"Romance Is Dying, Here's How to Save It," with Diana Kirschner, psychologist, bestselling author, and PBS love expert, November 24, 2018.

"Saying 'I Do' at Midlife," with Lauren Petkin, family attorney; and Virginia Gilbert, marriage and family therapist, June 24, 2019.

"Sex and the Single Girl," with Vanessa Marin, sex therapist, April 28, 2018.

"Sex, Marriage and Rock 'n' Roll," with John Cowsill and Vicki Peterson, married rock stars, May 23, 2019.

"Single at Midlife: What Every Woman Should Know," with Sandy Weiner, dating coach; and Silke Schwarzkopf, creator and host of 2nd Act TV, April 5, 2019.

"(Single) Parenting in a Pandemic," with Kristin MacDermott, resilience expert, October 16, 2020.

"Smarter Sex," with Susan Bratton, sex educator, author, and intimacy expert; and Jim Benson, men's sex and relationship coach, September 15, 2018.

"So You Want to Be in a Relationship?," with Jonathan Robinson, psychotherapist and author, April 21, 2018.

"Stop Choking Under Pressure and Start Dating with Confidence," with Aimee Daramus, clinical psychologist and professor, September 13, 2019.

"Stop Dating Your Unresolved Issues," with Crystal Jackson, blogger, August 1, 2019.

"Suddenly Single, Now What?," with Lauren Frances, love coach and author, May 7, 2019.

"Support Can Be Beautiful," with Nina Lorez-Collins and Hillary Richard, founders of The Woolfer, online platform for women over 40, January 22, 2019.

"Surviving Breakup Hell," with Fran Walfish, child and family psychotherapist; and Michelle Afont, divorce attorney, July 7, 2018.

"The 4 Habits of All Successful Relationships," with Andrea Cummings and Jon Taylor-Cummings, cofounders of Soul Mates Academy, November 15, 2019.

"The Best/Worst Dating Advice You're Ever Going to Get," with Karin Anderson Abrell, psychology professor, podcaster, and author, January 27, 2019.

"The Gloves Are Off: How to Fight Right," with Dave Gerber, conflict healer; and Lesley Aldermann, psychotherapist and writer, October 27, 2018.

"The 'It Factor' and How to Get It," with Suneel Gupta, professor, entrepreneur, and author, February 19, 2021.

"The Magic Is in You," with Arielle Ford, personal growth expert and author, September 8, 2018.

"The Secret to Love No One Will Tell You (but Arielle Ford Will)," with Arielle Ford, relationship expert and bestselling author, August 26, 2019.

"The Surprising Secret About Habits You Need to Know," with BJ Fogg, behavioral scientist and bestselling author, April 3, 2020.

"The Surprising Truth About Masculinity," with John Kim, author and therapist, June 27, 2019.

"The Woman Whisperer," with Ken Bechtel, relationship expert, September 29, 2018.

"To Swipe or Not to Swipe," with Julie Spira, digital dating expert, November 8, 2019.

"We've Got Your Valentine's Ideas Right Here," with Bob Cranston, wine expert; Jonathan Grahm, Compartes Chocolatier; Hanah An, owner of Crustacean; Lizzy Shaw, jeweler; Frank Parr, Peninsula Hotel; and Pamela Appleby, travel agent, February 8, 2019.

"What Does 'Doing the Work' Really Mean?," with Bex Burton, women's love coach; and Karyn Weiss, empowered single woman, October 18, 2019.

"What Triggers You?," with Veronica Grant, love and life coach, September 27, 2019.

"What Women Really Want," with anonymous single women, August 4, 2018.

"When Quitting Is the Best Thing You Can Do," with Dr. Stanley Robertson, author, coach, and speaker, October 11, 2019.

"Who Needs Marriage Anyway?," with Susan Pease Gadoua, psychotherapist and bestselling author, November 17, 2018.

"Who's Got the Power?," with Suzanne Oshima, life and love transformational coach, December 20, 2019.

"Who Will You Be After Coronavirus?," with Kathi Sharpe-Ross, public relations specialist and author, May 1, 2020.

"Why Do the Best of Us Get Dumped?," with Renee Slansky, dating and relationship coach, June 7, 2019.

# ACKNOWLEDGMENTS

I joked earlier that it took a village to get me married. Well, it turns out it took a village to write this book. It took a village of family, friends, mentors, bosses, clients, colleagues, ex-boyfriends, besties, acquaintances, and people I met along the way to get me here. From Beverly Vista to Beverly High, college to New York, and back to LA, you all had a hand in making this memoir.

Thank you to my village—the people who knew me when, the people who still refer to my father as Captain Groovy, the people who made me who I am today: a late-blooming, self-help author. They say that old friends are the best friends, but so are new friends, and you're all precious to me. Thank you for being with me on this ride; through thick and thin, good times and bad. Your loyalty is everything, your friendship is sustenance, and your spirit is throughout this book. Thank you also for embracing Robby. He loves you as much as I do.

Memoir writing is hard, but cathartic. It's exciting, but scary. It forces you to go deep and face the hard truths about yourself (which I'm a big fan of, as you know), then bring those truths out for all to see. Talk about vulnerability! But talk about empowering too! Delivering this book to my publishers was the most terrifying, yet bravest thing I've ever done. Actually no, giving the early draft to Robby to proofread was the most terrifying thing I've ever done because even he didn't know some things about me. Delving into your past and writing about it will give you gastritis and make you sweat, just like falling in love, which I used to think was death-defying until I wrote a memoir.

Robby once gave me a card with a quote that said: "Everything you want is on the other side of fear." I have it pinned up on my bulletin board as a reminder of what I can accomplish if I face my fears. That's exactly what I did to create these pages. Every day, hours a day, I sat at my computer and went to the other side of fear. And I'm so glad I did. Writing my story was powerful medicine, and a highly therapeutic exercise in self-discovery. Even if I don't sell a single copy of this book, it was still worth the experience.

If writing a memoir is hard, writing acknowledgments is crazy hard because I have more than a half a century of people to acknowledge. So, get comfortable because this may take a while. If I've left someone out, or forgot to mention you, please don't take it personally. Blame it on menopausal brain fog.

To anyone and everyone on social media who shared my blogs, podcasts, and other content, I know who you are, and I thank you for sharing the love! Many thanks to Dick and Sharon Price at L.A. Progressive/Hollywood Progressive, for getting on board early with my blogs, and to Silke Schwarzkopf of 2nd Act TV, who literally put me on the map. Thank you for being such a great friend and fan.

To our *Done Being Single* listeners, many thanks for tuning in and being so generous with your praise and support.

I'd like to thank my team at Greenleaf Book Group for a great publishing experience: David Endris, Leah Pierre, Sally Garland, Elizabeth Brown, Anne Sanow, Cameron Stein, Valerie Howard, and Chelsea Richards. Unlike losing my real virginity, losing my first-time author virginity to you felt really good. Your guidance, ideas, and expertise were so pleasurable, I just might do it again with you.

Before I got to Greenleaf, I had the pleasure of working with two fantastic editors, Shawna Kenney, and the late, great Jane Gassner, who told me years ago that my blogs could become a book. Jane was a tough customer who cracked the whip and made me a better writer. RIP Jane.

To my track coach, Chuck Kloes: I'll never forgive you for yanking me out of the 300 low hurdles and putting me in the 440, but I thank you for doing it. Turning me into a quarter-miler gave me grit for the road ahead.

Using a favorite betting term, I hit a two-team parlay with Kathie Sharpe Ross: She's not only a book maven, she's one of my besties, too. Thanks Mo, for your publishing prowess and friendship. You're a pro at both!

To my former fitness clients, thank you for welcoming me into your hearts and gyms, and becoming dear friends while we were at it. You trusted me with your bodies and allowed me to do cruel and unusual things to you. I miss you terribly, but I don't miss getting up at the crack of dawn to train you. Heartfelt appreciation and kudos to my life and dating coaching clients for putting up with my tough love and allowing me to join them on their journeys. It continues to be an honor helping you find love, purpose, and the path forward.

Huge gratitude to my spiritual dream team: Spencer Grendahl, Kit Wilkins, and Catherine Weissenberg. You're all an incredible guiding force in my life. To Karen Page, is it any wonder your Moon conjuncts my Sun? No one gets me more than you. I love you so much.

To my mah-jongg sisters, aka the Mahj Tribunal, aka Hel's Angels (named after our esteemed mah-jongg teacher Helaine), thank you for your spirit and support. You got me through some hella shitty times with love, laughter, wine, song, and a few games of Mahj too (yes, readers, we drink and sing while we play). You're the wind beneath my wings and the Jokers in my rack. Rack 'em up! To my tennis friends, I owe you a debt of gratitude for keeping me on your roster and in the loop. Doesn't matter if I play deuce or ad, I just love being on the court with you.

Many thanks to my friends who gave my single life, life. You kept me company, fed me, fixed me up, gave me shoulders to cry on, and never judged. Well, some of you judged, and I needed it. Without your tough love, I'd still be with that guy you hated.

To my ex-boyfriends, thanks and sorry. Sometimes it was you, sometimes it was me, and now we can all hug it out. To my sperm donors—known and unknown—it probably wasn't you, it was most likely me, but I thank you anyway for trying to make my dream come true. Your jizz will forever be in my heart.

I may be an only child, but as mentioned, I have a huge extended family of cousins that must be thanked for their love and support: Estelle, Jew-Lo, and Randy; Rona and Derek; David and Fern; Anita and Charlie; Michael, Sharon, Jeanna, and BoBo; Mark, Kayla, Darin, Dirk, and Jenny; Day-Lo, Tracy, and Ian;

Darren, Lisa, Evan, Devyn, Trevor, Calum, Eric, and Stephanie; Tobias, Nicolas, Calva, Sophie, Jenna, Chloe, Sophie, Benjamin, and Hannah. You are truly the gift that keeps on giving, and you keep multiplying! Here's to the Watchman clan, long may we reign! All hail my Zilz family stepcousins too!

Now that I'm married, my circle of friends and family has grown. Much love to my sisters-in-law Wendy and JuJu, and their families. To Robby's father Eddie, who was like a second dad to me, and Fran, whom I never knew, but know I would love (and hope she would love me too), thank you for producing the most extraordinary human being and husband in Robby. To Robby's pals, thank you for embracing me, and to Robby's ex-girlfriends, thanks for delivering him to me. You did a great job; I'll take it from here.

To my parents, Paul and Sonjia, aka Pops and Yo-Yo, I'm going to make this short or else I'll start crying. You were with me in every chapter, on every page, and in everything I do in life. I love you for all the incredible things you gave me, except for your high cholesterol, for which I'm now taking Lipitor. To Suzanne and Stacy, thanks for taking such good care of my father. He would end every phone call with me by saying "Madly," which was code for "I love you." Madly to you both.

To everyone in the Commercials Unlimited family, who knew and worked with Sonjia over the years, including staff, agents, and clients, thank you. You meant the world to her. Tim and Janie Allen, no one loved you more than Sonjia, although I'm a close second.

Finally, to Robby, I'm so glad you were done being single. Thank you for giving me this beautiful story to tell. You are this book, my life, and the loviest love that ever was!

# ABOUT THE AUTHOR

Treva Brandon Scharf is a multi-hyphenate: ICF-certified life, dating, relationship coach, fitness professional, midlife marriage first-timer, late bloomer, memoirist, and self-help author.

Her dating advice has been featured in the *Huffington Post, Hollywood/ LA Progressive,* Ariana Huffington's *Thrive Global, The Intelligencer, Bustle, Upjourney, BetterAfter50,* and many other publications.

Treva is an advocate for strong, independent singles, an empowered voice for women of all ages, and a champion of late bloomers everywhere.